Fashionable Projects for the New Knitter

Fashionable Projects for the New Knitter

ALISON BARLOW

Sterling Publishing Co., Inc. New York
A Sterling/Chapelle Book

Chapelle, Ltd.

P.O. Box 9252, Ogden, UT 84409

(801) 621-2777 • (801) 621-2788 Fax

e-mail: chapelle@chapelleltd.com

Web site: www.chapelleltd.com

Library of Congress Cataloging-in-Publication Data

Barlow, Alison.

  Fashionable projects for the new knitter / Alison Barlow.

      p. cm.

  Includes index.

  ISBN-13: 978-1-4027-3070-2

  ISBN-10: 1-4027-3070-5

1. Knitting--Patterns. I. Title.

TT820.B175 2006

746.43'2041--dc22

                                                            2005032986

10 9 8 7 6 5 4 3 2 1

Published by Sterling Publishing Co., Inc.

387 Park Avenue South, New York, NY 10016

©2006 by Alison Barlow

Distributed in Canada by Sterling Publishing

% Canadian Manda Group, 165 Dufferin Street

Toronto, Ontario, Canada M6K 3H6

Distributed in the United Kingdom by GMC Distribution Services,

Castle Place, 166 High Street, Lewes, East Sussex, England BN7 1XU

Distributed in Australia by Capricorn Link (Australia) Pty. Ltd.

P.O. Box 704, Windsor, NSW 2756, Australia

Printed and Bound in China

All Rights Reserved

Sterling ISBN-13: 978-1-4027-3070-2

        ISBN-10: 1-4027-3070-5

For information about custom editions, special sales, premium and corporate purchases, please contact Sterling Special Sales Department at 800-805-5489 or specialsales@sterlingpub.com.

contents

introduction

I have fond memories, from my days as a young girl, of my Grandma Millie's and my mother's knitting group. Each Wednesday, they met at Minnie Richards's house, where they would make the most fabulous articles of clothing. My mom and Grandma Millie were prolific knitters, but I never felt like knitting was my "thing" until years later.

In 1995, my mom opened The Wool Cabin, a yarn shop in Salt Lake City, Utah. She thought it would be great if I came to the shop one day a week to bring her lunch, or maybe straighten out some yarn for her. Before long, I could see the appeal—so many great fibers, my mom helping out knitters with their projects, and the wonderful camaraderie with one another. I found myself picking out yarn, needles, and instructions for my very first project—a baby blanket. Shortly thereafter, I had several projects going, was working in the shop two days a week, and had discovered my own healthy addiction to knitting.

Knitting is the craft of making fabric by interlocking small loops of yarn. Each time a loop is pulled through another loop on a set of knitting needles, one stitch is formed. The stitches are worked between needles, creating a supple fabric from lengths of yarn.

Although it is not known exactly when or where knitting was developed, it is clearly an old craft. The first known references to knitting date back to the early 14th century, although it is entirely possible that it had been in existence for centuries prior. With the Industrial Revolution, knitting experienced somewhat of a decline as machines in factories were capable of creating knitted items very quickly. In recent years, however, knitting has become extremely popular once again.

This book is intended to teach the beginner through projects that introduce new stitches and knitting techniques as you go. In these pages, you will find manageable projects that will help you become familiar with the process and rhythm of knitting and will give you a sense of accomplishment. I recommend that you follow the projects sequentially in order to more easily build upon your knowledge and use what you are learning as you create.

general instructions

TOOLS AND MATERIALS

Needles

Choosing the right needles for a project can be difficult for a beginner, because there are so many types available. Each of the projects in this book will list the type of needle to be used; however, here is some basic information that may be helpful in the future.

Straight needles are the most basic. Circular needles can be used for the same projects as straight needles, but will accommodate more stitches. They can also be used to knit cylindrical objects, as long as the project is not smaller in circumference than the needle. Double-pointed needles are also used to knit in the round; however, the size of the project is not dependent on the size of the needle.

The size of a knitting needle is based on diameter. Thinner needles have smaller numbers; for example, a size 0 needle has a much smaller diameter than a size 17. Needle lengths also vary, depending on the project at hand.

Knitting needles are manufactured in aluminum, steel, wood, and plastic. There is very little functional difference between material; it is generally a matter of personal preference.

Yarns

Yarn can be purchased in a ball, hank, or skein, and is measured by yardage when determining how much is required for a particular project. The yardage varies by manufacturer, and the projects throughout this book will list the necessary number of yarn units and yarn weight.

It is important to know the gauge or tension of the yarn in order to correctly size a project. Gauge indicates the number of stitches and rows that will be yielded per inch of yarn, and is determined by the gauge of the

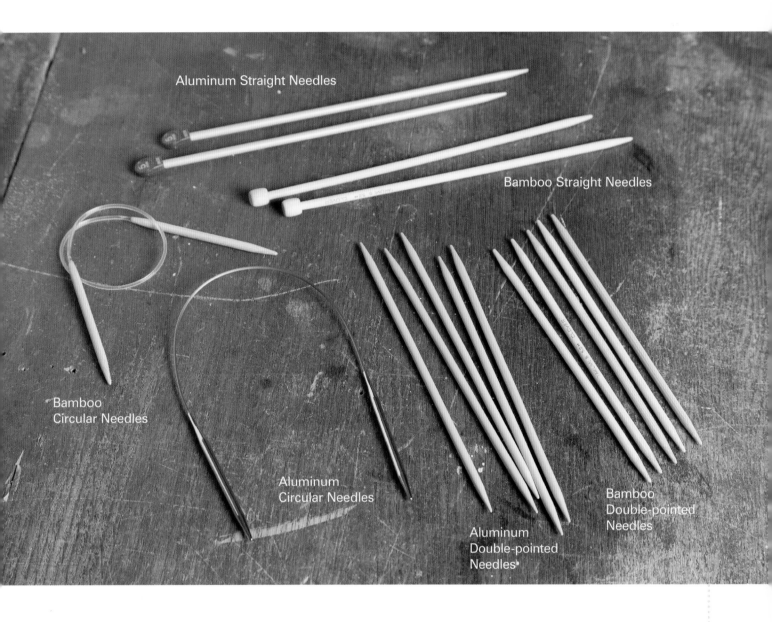

Aluminum Straight Needles

Bamboo Straight Needles

Bamboo
Circular Needles

Aluminum
Circular Needles

Aluminum
Double-pointed
Needles

Bamboo
Double-pointed
Needles

needles

The main difference between
aluminum and bamboo needles
is the way they feel in your hands.

yarn and the size of the needles being used; however, this does not mean that all yarns with the same gauge are created equal. For example, two yarns that both produce five stitches per inch on size 7 needles may drape differently, or have very distinct textures. Novelty yarns do not generally have a gauge, and will therefore not be listed when used in projects throughout this book.

Yarn weights refer to the thickness of the strand of yarn, which largely determines its gauge. For example, a medium-weight yarn may have a gauge of five stitches and seven rows to the inch. However, a heavy- or bulky-weight yarn, when worked on the same size needles, may only work up three stitches and five rows to the inch. Thus, it will take less knitting with the bulky yarn than the medium-weight yarn to stitch the same number of inches.

While there are no standardized categories for yarn weights, there are generalized terms that describe yarns by thickness and size of needle they are usually worked on. The label on the yarn will have this information (see Fig.1).

Yarn	Needles	Stitches per Inch
Baby/Fingering	1–3	7–8
Double Knit (DK) or Sport	3–6	5–6
Worsted	5–7	5
Chunky	7–9	4–5
Bulky	10–11	2–3

Fig. 1

Worsted

Baby/Fingering

Bulky

Chunky

Double Knit

yarns

Yarns are classed by their weight, or strand thickness. This determines their gauge, or the number of stitches per inch they will yield.

Other Tools and Materials

Buttons: Used as embellishments or serving a functional purpose, buttons are occasionally called for in some of the projects in this book.

Cable needle: This is a special needle used specifically for creating cables in knitted items.

Crochet hook: Crochet hooks are very useful for picking up dropped stitches, correcting minor errors, and making yarn ends inconspicuous by threading them through the project.

Safety pins: Safety pins can be used as a marker for dropped stitches.

Scissors: A good sharp pair of craft scissors will be necessary for cutting.

Stitch holder: Shaped like a large safety pin, a stitch holder is meant to keep stitches safely while the needles are being used for something else. The stitches can later be transferred back to a needle when ready to be knit again.

Stitch markers: Stitch markers are small plastic rings that are helpful in remembering where rows begin when knitting the round.

Tapestry needle: A blunt-tip, large-eyed tapestry needle is necessary for sewing pieces together.

tip

Look for scissors with a rounded tip for those times when you want to take your knitting with you when you are traveling.

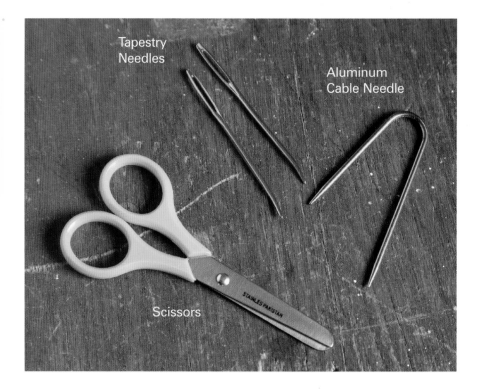

Tapestry Needles

Aluminum Cable Needle

Scissors

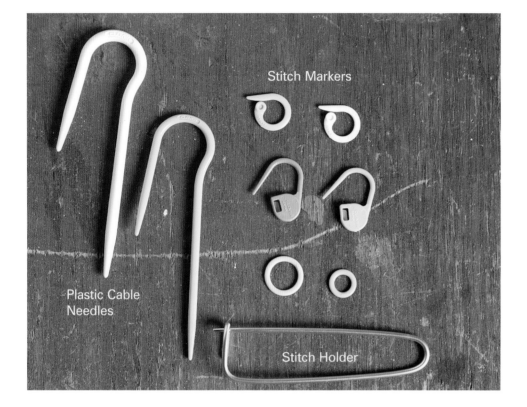

Stitch Markers

Plastic Cable Needles

Stitch Holder

READING PATTERNS AND INSTRUCTIONS

Oftentimes, patterns use a number of abbreviations and knitting terms. Here is a short glossary of abbreviations and terms:

beg:	begin(ning)	**psso:**	pass slip stitch over	**place marker on needle:**	put a ring or loop of colored yarn on needle to separate stitches
bo:	bind off	**rnd(s):**	round(s) (circular row)		
co:	cast on	**RS:**	right side		
dec:	decrease(s) (ing)	**sl:**	slip		
dp:	double pointed	**sl st:**	slip stitch	**place marker in work:**	use a safety pin or strand of yarn to mark a stitch or row
k:	knit(ed) (ing) (garter)	**ssk:**	slip, slip, knit.		
k2tog:	knit 2 stitches together as one	**st(s):**	stitch(es)		
		tog:	together	**turn work:**	turn piece around so back of work on previous row is now toward you
inc:	increase(s) (ing)	**WS:**	wrong side		
lp(s):	loop(s)	**yo:**	yarn over		
p:	purl(ing)	**⁕:**	repeat as indicated	**work even:**	work without decreasing or increasing
p2tog:	purl 2 stitches together as one				

Skein of Yarn

Hank of Yarn

KNITTING BASICS

The most basic of all knitting stitches are called "knit" and "purl." These two stitches can create hundreds of patterns when combined in various ways. The next few pages will illustrate how to cast on, create knit and purl stitches, and bind off. Included in this section are trouble-shooting and "fix it" techniques for dropped stitches.

Preparing Yarn for Knitting

The preparation of the yarn will depend on whether it is a ball, a hank, or a skein.

Ball of Yarn

Yarn wound in a ball can be pulled from the center or unrolled from the outside.

Hank of Yarn

Yarn in a hank is wound in a large circle that is then twisted and knotted together at the ends. This makes pulling yarn directly from the hank nearly impossible. Before beginning to knit, unfold the hank of yarn into a large circle. Have a friend hold the circle on both ends, then wind the yarn into a ball.

Skein of Yarn

If the yarn is in a skein, you can simply pull the end of the yarn from the center and start knitting.

Casting On (co)

The term "casting on" simply means placing the first row of loops onto a knitting needle, which provides the foundation for the entire project.

1. Measure off a length of yarn, leaving about 1" per st that will be co.

2. Make a slipknot.

    a. Loosely wrap the yarn around the index and middle fingers of your left hand (see Fig. 2).

    b. Pull the yarn coming from the skein up through the lp (see Fig. 3).

    c. Tighten the lp by lightly pulling on the tail of the yarn, creating the slipknot (see Fig. 4 on page 18).

3. Insert a knitting needle through the lp, so that the tip points left (see Fig. 5 on page 18).

4. With the needle in your right hand, wrap the tail end of the yarn around your left thumb. Wrap the yarn from the skein over your left index finger, securing both pieces of yarn between palm and remaining fingers.

5. Insert needle tip under the thumb lp, then up and over the index-finger lp. Use the needle tip to draw the yarn from the skein through the thumb lp to form a new st (see Fig. 6 on page 18).

6. Sl thumb out of lp. Lightly pull the tail end of the yarn to secure the lp to the needle (see Fig. 7 on page 18).

7. Repeat Steps 3–5 for remaining sts.

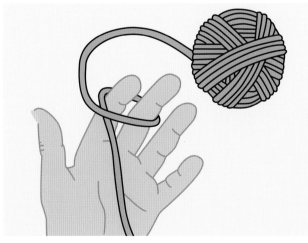

Fig. 2

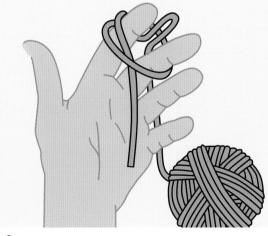

Fig. 3

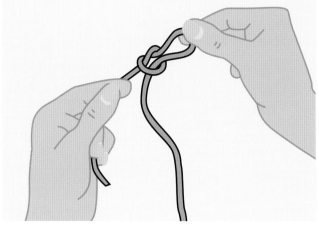

Fig. 4

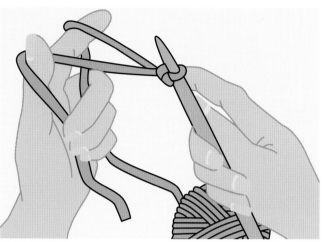

Fig. 5

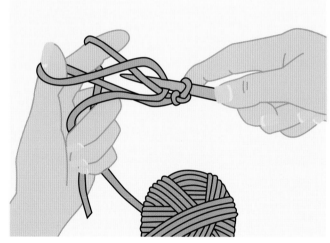

Fig. 6

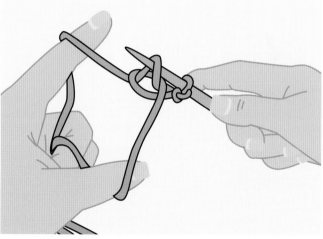

Fig. 7

Holding the Yarn and Needles

Knitting may feel a bit awkward when first beginning. However, it will become more comfortable over time, especially if good habits are acquired early on.

1. Simply hold the needle with the co sts in your left hand, so that your palm and fingers support the needle (see Fig. 8).

2. To maintain the correct amount of tension, wind the yarn around the fingers of your right hand. It should drape over the index finger, go under the middle and ring fingers, and around the pinky (see Fig. 9). *Note: Tension is imperative to creating sts that are neither too tight nor too loose.*

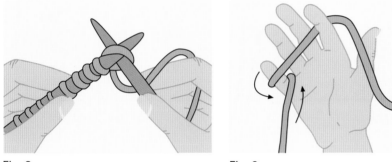

Fig. 8   Fig. 9

Garter (Knit) Stitch (k)

Now that the yarn is cast onto the first needle and you can keep proper tension, it is time to learn how to create all subsequent rows.

1. Insert the second needle through the first st, so that the right-hand needle is behind the left-hand needle (see Fig. 10).

2. Using right index finger, wrap the yarn coming from the skein around the back of the right-hand needle, and bring down between the two knitting needles. Make certain the yarn is coming from behind (see Fig. 11).

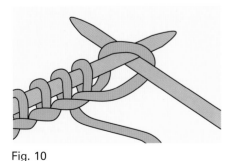

Fig. 10   Fig. 11

An example of the garter stitch.

19

3. Bring the right-hand needle down in front of the left-hand needle, and move the st from the left-hand needle to the right-hand needle (see Figs. 12 and 13).

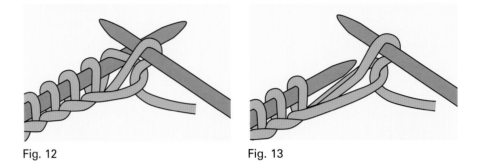

Fig. 12   Fig. 13

4. Repeat through the end of the row, moving sts down the right needle and up the left needle as necessary. *Note: Once all of the sts have been transferred to the other needle, one row has been completed.*

5. Make certain to count your sts at the end of each row to ensure that no sts have been inadvertently dropped or added.

6. Repeat Steps 1–5 for as many rows as the pattern calls for, or as many rows as you like.

The pattern produced by knitting every row is called a garter (k) stitch. Both sides of the knitted fabric are identical, with a bumpy texture. Unlike some other stitch patterns, the garter stitch does not curl along the edges. Oftentimes, written knitting instructions will refer to "ridges" instead of rows when working in a garter stitch, as the ridges are easier to count (see Fig. 14).

The garter stitch is used in the Garter Stitch Bag on pages 76–77.

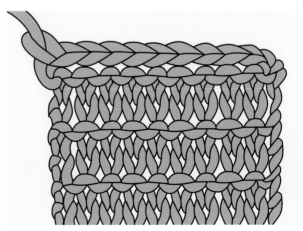

Fig. 14

Purl Stitch (p)

A purl stitch is basically a backward knit stitch. If all rows are purled, the pattern will look exactly like a garter stitch. It is to be assumed that anytime a pattern asks for a garter stitch, that all rows are to be knitted, unless otherwise specified. Purl stitches have a very bumpy look to them, and are very easy to learn. Simply cast on the desired number of stitches, and follow these instructions.

1. With the yarn in front of the work, insert right-hand needle tip into the first st on the left-hand needle, from front to back (see Fig. 15).

2. Pull yarn to front of the work, pass it counterclockwise behind and around the right-hand needle tip, and return it to the front of the work (see Fig. 16).

3. Sl right-hand needle out from original st (see Fig. 17).

4. With new lp on right-hand needle, sl left-hand needle out of original st (see Fig. 18).

5. Repeat Steps 1–3 through end of row.

An example of the purl stitch.

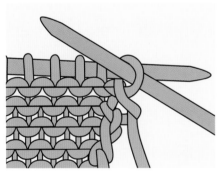

Fig. 15

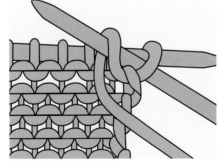

Fig. 16

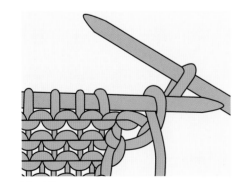

Fig. 17

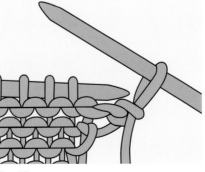

Fig. 18

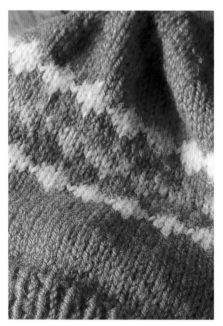

An example of the stockinette stitch.

Stockinette Stitch (stockinette st)

The stockinette stitch is a simple pattern that will produce repeating "V"s on the knit side of the work, and bumpy ridges on the purl side.

1. To create the stockinette st, simply k every other row and p every other row (see Fig. 19).

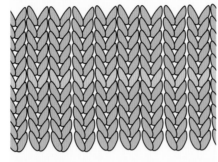

Fig. 19

An example of the seed stitch.

Seed Stitch (seed st)

The seed stitch creates a pattern that is sometimes described as a "checkerboard." It is created by purling the knit stitches and knitting the purl stitches.

1. *K1, p1* through end of row.

2. On the second row *p1, k1* through end of row. *Note: By co an even number of sts, every other row will beg with a k st, while rows in between will beg with a p st. However, by co an odd number of sts, every row will beg with a k st, eliminating the need to check the direction of the first st when each new row is begun.*

3. Repeat Steps 1–2 for desired number of rows.

Slip Stitch (sl st)

1. If the instructions call for a sl st, simply sl the st from the left-hand needle to the right, without actually k a new st (see Fig. 20). *Note: This will create a more even edge in many cases.*

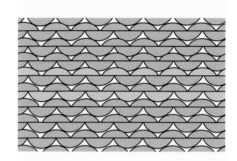

Fig. 20

Yarn Over (yo)

A yarn over will add an extra stitch to the right-hand needle, and is a method for increasing.

1. Bring yarn forward into p st position. Sl the right-hand needle into the st in the regular k st position.

2. Bring the yarn up and around, between the two needles. K the st (see Fig. 21).

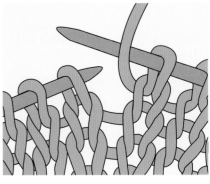
Fig. 21

Increasing (inc)

Although the yarn over method works well for increasing, there are other ways in which it can be accomplished.

1. To k an inc, beg to k1 as usual; however, make certain not to sl the st off of the left-hand needle (see Fig. 22).

2. Insert the right-hand needle behind the left again, and k1, sl st off left-hand needle this time (see Fig. 23). *Note: This creates an added st on the right-hand needle.*

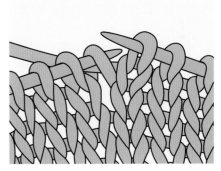
Fig. 22

Kitchener Stitch (kitchener st)

The kitchener stitch is useful for sewing together sweater or sock seams. When done properly, the seam is nearly invisible. Simply follow these steps (see Fig. 24):

Hold the two needles in left hand with points facing right.

1. Thread a large tapestry needle with yarn and sl through the first st on front needle as if to p. Leave st on needle.

2. Draw the yarn through the first st on back needle as if to k. Leave st on needle.

3. Draw the yarn through the first st on the front needle, as if to k, and sl it off needle.

4. Draw the yarn through the next st on the front needle, as if to p. Leave st on needle.

5. Draw the yarn through the first st on the back needle, as if to p, and sl it off needle.

6. Draw the yarn through the next st on the back needle, as if to k. Leave st on needle.

7. Repeat Steps 3–6 until all sts are off the needles.

8. Weave in ends.

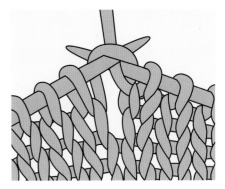
Fig. 23

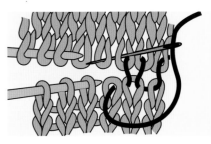
Fig. 24

Fig. 25

Fig. 26

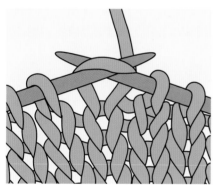

Fig. 27

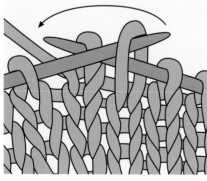

Fig. 28

Slip, Slip, Knit (ssk)

This is a method for working two stitches together as one. It mirrors the k2tog, and prevents the stitches from turning out backward when decreasing.

1. Sl 2 sts from the left-hand needle to the right-hand needle without k (see Fig. 25).

2. Insert tip of left needle in front of both sl sts, as if p backward (see Fig. 26).

3. Wrap the yarn around the right-hand needle tip and k the 2 sl sts tog.

Pass Slip Stitch Over (psso)

Passing a slipped stitch over is a method for decreasing at a slant. It maintains a particular pattern when knitting.

1. K1.

2. Insert needle into next st as if to k and transfer to right-hand needle without k (see Fig. 27).

3. Without untwisting the sts, sl them back onto the left-hand needle. Pass the sl st over the k st and off the needle (see Fig. 28). *Note: This same technique can be applied for p, simply by sl the st as if to p.*

Cable

Although knitting cables might seem intimidating, it is actually quite a simple process.

1. Simply sl the required number of sts to a cable needle, and hold in front of or behind the work, depending on whether the pattern calls for a front cable (fc) or a back cable (bc).

2. K the required number of subsequent sts on the left-hand needle as always, then k the sts directly off of the cable needle. *Note: This causes the sts to crossover, creating the cable. For example, if the pattern says p1, fc3, p1, simply p1 st, sl 3 sts to the cable needle and hold in front, k3 sts from the left-hand needle, k the 3 sts directly off of the cable needle, then p1 st from the left-hand needle.*

Starting/Joining a New Skein of Yarn

If you find you are running out of one skein of yarn and need to start a fresh one, there are a couple of ways to do this.

The first and preferred method is to end with the old skein at the end of a WS row. Do not worry about using up all the yarn on this skein. It is better to break off and set aside a bit of yarn than to arrive at its end in the middle of a row or on the RS of the pattern. Leave a long enough tail to work with, but not so long that it will be mistaken for the working yarn. Start the new skein at the beginning of the next row and again leave a tail (see Fig. 29). Tie the two tails into a square knot (right over left, left over right) and leave the ends for weaving into the knitting later.

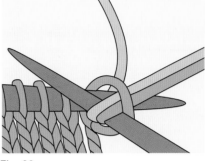

Fig. 29

The second method is to leave a tail from the yarn in the first skein wherever its end may fall, pick up the second skein and, leaving a tail from it also, knit the next couple of stitches (see Fig. 30). Go back and tie the two ends in a square knot and weave the ends in later. Try to keep the knot and the ends on the WS of the work.

If you come to a break in the yarn in the skein that was tied in a knot by the manufacturer, do not just knit it into the work as that knot will probably not hold. Untie or cut the knot out and retie it, using a square knot. Weave the ends into the piece later.

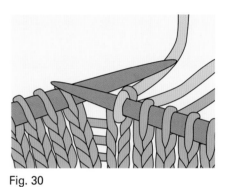

Fig. 30

Right Side (RS) versus Wrong Side (WS)

The terms right side (RS) and wrong side (WS) are often used in knitting patterns. Keeping track of the RS and WS is important in patterns that require shaping, as it is necessary to be consistent and work the proper stitches in the proper places. In stockinette, RS is generally the knit side and WS is the purl side. If using stitches that are reversible, such as garter or seed, simply place a safety pin on the side that will be designated RS.

tip

Do not let the needle penetrate the yarn being used. Some yarns, especially plied ones, are prone to splitting. Make certain to go in and out of the holes in the stitches, leaving the yarn strand intact.

KNITTING IN THE ROUND

"Knitting in the round," or knitting every row in a circle, is a very useful method for making hats and other tubular pieces when you do not want to have a seam. Despite never purling a single stitch, knitting in the round will produce the stockinette pattern. There are two ways to knit in the round: using circular needles or double-pointed needles.

Circular Needles

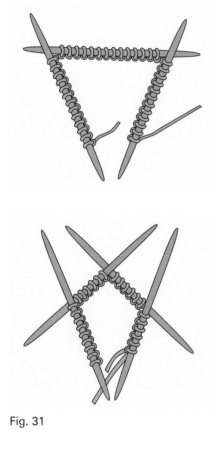

In order to knit on circular needles, the circumference of the needles must be smaller than the circumference of the object being knit. For example, if the hat will be 25" around, using 28" needles will not be possible. However, the instructions for projects requiring circular needles will specify the necessary length. Always make certain your stitches are not twisted. Nothing can untwist them!

1. Co as usual. Place the needle with the long end of yarn and last co st in the right hand, and the needle with the very first co st in the left hand.

2. Beg k as usual, so that the first and last sts are joined tog in a circle.

Double-pointed Needles

Just about any size garment can be knitted on any size double-pointed needle, aside from a very large circle knitted on very short needles.

1. Beg by co the required number of sts onto one of the dp needles.

2. Depending on the size of the garment, divide the number of sts evenly onto three or four dp needles. To do this, simply sl subsequent sts, as though k a p st, from one needle to the next (see Fig. 31).

3. The first co st should be at the end of the left-hand needle, while the last co st is at the end of the right-hand needle. Beg k as usual. *Note: This will create a tube shape as all of the sts are transferred around. However, make certain to beg with the open end of the needles in front, because if you beg with the center needle, the tube will be k inside out.*

Fig. 31

FINISHING

Use the following methods for finishing an individual piece of knitted fabric and for burying remaining yarn ends and tails in the work.

Binding Off (bo)

Binding, or casting, off is the term used for removing needles from the knitted project without the entire piece unraveling.

1. K2 at the beg of the row (see Fig. 32).

2. Sl the first st over the second st. Remove the overlapping st, so the second st remains on the needle (see Fig. 33).

3. K1, repeat Step 2.

4. Repeat Steps 1–3 until the last st is bo.

5. Cut a short tail and pull it through the last st. The tail can then be woven through the k fabric (see Fig. 34).

 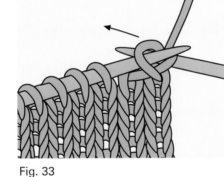 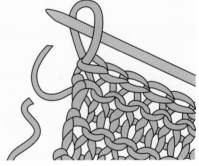

Fig. 32   Fig. 33   Fig. 34

Weaving in Yarn Ends and Tails

Upon completing a knitted piece, you will likely find that there are several yarn ends that need to be woven into the piece before you can begin sewing up seams or assembling pieces together.

1. Using a tapestry needle, weave in all ends and tails back through completed k about 3" deep and cut off excess (see Fig. 35).

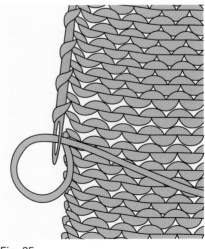

Fig. 35

CORRECTING ERRORS

Troubleshooting

Although knitting is relatively easy, mistakes are inevitable and repairs may need to be made in the course of completing a project.

For example, when moving a project from place to place between knitting sessions, it is possible for the needle to slip out of the stitches. Or, during knitting, a stitch can be accidentally dropped off the needle, leaving a hole in the cloth that will eventually cause the piece to unravel. Or, you may make a mistake and not discover it until long after it is made, requiring that you take out several rows to fix it.

As you begin knitting, it may be helpful to check your work by counting the stitches after each row. One stitch more or less than you cast on means that something is wrong in the last row worked. After awhile, counting stitches will not be necessary. Your fingers will alert you to a missed move, and you will be catching mistakes before you have proceeded too far in your project.

If you count the number of stitches on the knitting needle and discover that you have one stitch less than you should have, you have probably dropped a stitch. Carefully spread out the stitches along the needle and slowly scan the row(s) below the needle until the dropped stitch is located. Carefully work the tip of a safety pin into the dropped stitch, securing and stretching it out. Refer to the correct method for retrieving the dropped stitch.

Correcting a Dropped Stitch

The method used to correct a dropped stitch depends on whether you want to knit the stitch or purl it. The unworked horizontal strand of yarn will either be behind or in front of the dropped stitch. If there is no sign of an unknitted strand, place the stitch back on the left-hand needle.

tip

Pick up the strands of yarn in the proper order. Pulling a loop through from a strand in the wrong row will cause more problems.

Knitting a Dropped Stitch

If the purl side is facing you or you are working in the garter stitch, correct the dropped stitch as follows:

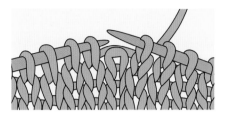

1. Insert right-hand needle tip into front of dropped (pinned) st. *Note: If you look behind the st, you will notice a horizontal strand of yarn that did not get wrapped and pulled through as a new st.*

2. Move the right-hand needle tip under this unworked strand from the front, placing the strand and the st on the needle (see Fig. 36).

3. Insert the left-hand needle into the st from the back and pull it over the strand. *Note: The strand has become a st.*

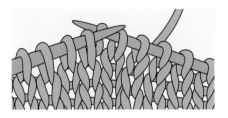

4. Place the new st on the left-hand needle. Make certain that you have made a smooth V st. Continue working the pattern as indicated.

Purling a Dropped Stitch

If the purl side is facing or you are working in stockinette stitch, correct the dropped stitch as follows.

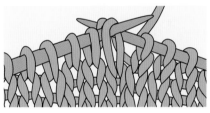

1. Insert the right-hand needle tip into the dropped st and the unworked strand from the back. *Note: If you look in front of the st you will see a horizontal strand of yarn that did not get wrapped and pulled through as a new st.*

Fig. 36

2. Using the left-hand needle, pull the dropped st over the strand and off the needle, forming a new st on the right-hand needle (see Fig. 37).

3. Place the new st on the left-hand needle. Continue working the pattern as indicated.

Correcting a Dropped Stitch in a Row Below

If you notice a dropped stitch in the row below, continue working until you reach the pinned stitch.

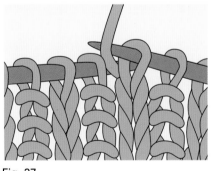

Fig. 37

Fig. 38

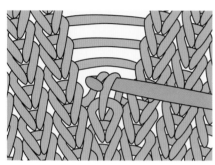

Fig. 39

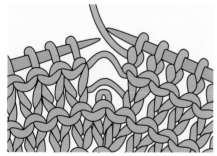

Fig. 40

Fig. 41

Correcting a Dropped Stitch from Several Rows Below

If the dropped stitch has worked itself down several rows, find the dropped stitch and secure it with a safety pin. Work to the stitch count where the stitch dropped. The wayward stitch will be at the bottom of a "ladder" of unworked strands. Each strand represents a row (see Fig. 38).

Correcting a Dropped Stitch in Stockinette Stitch

1. On the k side, use a crochet hook to come up through the pinned st. Pick up the bottom strand in the ladder.

2. Pull the strand through the st, forming a new st. (see Fig. 39) Continue to pull each strand in the ladder through the lp on the crochet hook until the last strand has been worked.

3. Pull on the work in each direction after correcting a dropped st to blend the sts.

4. Sl the last lp on the crochet hook back onto the left-hand k needle. Continue working the pattern as indicated.

Correcting a Dropped Stitch in Garter Stitch

1. On the p side, alternate the direction from which the ladder strands are pulled through the dropped st. Pull strand through the front of the st for a k st. Pull strand through the back of the st for a p st (see Figs. 40 and 41).

2. Determine whether to pull the first strand at the bottom ladder through the secured st from the front or the back. To do this, follow the bottom strand to the side to see what the st connected to it looks like. If necessary, pull gently on the strand to locate the neighboring sts.

Note: If the base of the next st is the bottom of a V, it is a k st and the dropped st should be picked up from the front. If the base st is a bump, insert the crochet hook into the st from back to front (toward you), pick up the strand, and pull it through. Make certain the rescued st matches the ones next to it or follows the established pattern.

3. Alternate pulling sts from each direction until the last strand has been pulled through. Put the last lp onto the left-hand k needle. Continue working as indicated.

Correcting Too Many Stitches

If too many stitches are on the needle, the yarn may have crossed the needle while you were not paying attention, inadvertently increasing the number of stitches or it could mean that the wrap of yarn has not quite made it through the old stitch. The stitch will need to be ripped out.

Ripping Out: Stitch by Stitch

If the mistake is on the row you are working, rip back one stitch at a time, using the following method:

1. With the k or p side facing, insert the left-hand needle tip from front to back into the st below the one on the right-hand needle (see Figs. 42 and 43).

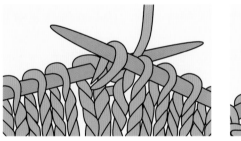 

Fig. 42   Fig. 43

2. Slide the right-hand needle out of the st and gently rip, or pull, the working yarn to undo the st.

3. Continue to rip back, st by st, to the point of the mistake. Continue working the pattern as indicated.

Ripping Out: Row by Row

1. If the mistake is located several rows below the one you are working, rip out the necessary rows by locating the row with the mistake and marking it with a safety pin.

2. Slide the k needles out of the sts. Gently rip, or pull, the working yarn to undo the sts, until you are on the row above the mistake. Rip to the end of the row.

Note: Gathering the work loosely in your left hand while gently pulling the yarn away will help keep the work from stretching and pulling other sts out.

tip

Use a needle several sizes smaller to pick up the last row of the ripped-out knitting. Change to the regular-sized needle when working the next row.

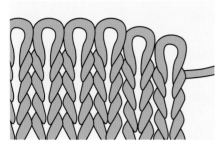

Fig. 44

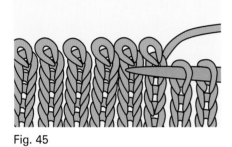

Fig. 45

An example of felted wool.

3. Hold your knitting with the working yarn on the right (flip it over if it is on the left). Insert the tip of the needle into the first st on the row below from back to front (toward you).

4. Pull on the yarn to unravel the st (see Fig. 44). Make certain to have 1 st on the right-hand needle. Continue to rip back, st by st, to the point of the mistake. Rip out the mistake. Continue working the pattern as indicated (see Fig. 45).

Occasionally, a mistake will be made while knitting; however, starting over is not usually an option. Follow the easy methods illustrated here and many mistakes will not be too difficult to fix.

FELTING

In the most straightforward of terms, "felting" is just creating matted wool. The process through which wool turns into felt is actually quite simple. When the wool is submerged in hot soapy water, it becomes very slippery. The tiny threads of fiber slide across each other and become tangled together. Once the wool dries, it shrinks into the tightly packed fabric we commonly know as felt.

Just about everyone has inadvertently felted a wool item. The tricky part to felting on purpose is estimating how much the wool will shrink, so that the item can be knitted to the proper size. The felted projects in this book have eliminated the guesswork; however, future projects may require a few sample squares, especially when using a new yarn. Remember that white wool will not felt.

1. Place knitted items into a mesh lingerie bag and put into washing machine.

2. Add a small amount of no-rinse wool soap or laundry detergent.

3. Using hot water and the smallest water level, begin the wash cycle.

4. Every few minutes, check the progress of the felt. If the items are of the desired size, remove the bag from the washer. If they need to shrink a bit more, continue washing.

5. Hand-rinse the felted items in water no cooler than the wash water.

6. Spin the items in the washer for 1–2 minutes or gently roll in a towel to remove excess water.

CORDS AND CONSTRUCTION

I-cord

The I-cord is made using double-pointed needles. It creates a tube, with the wrong side somewhat resembling a ladder, as the yarn is pulled across the back of the work (see Fig. 46).

1. Co sts onto dp needles.

2. Push sts to opposite end of needle. Make certain to not turn the needle around. K all sts.

3. Repeat Step 2 until piece is desired length.

4. Bo.

Fig. 46

Whipstitch

The whipstitch is very simple to do and can be done fairly quickly to sew two edges together (see Fig. 47).

1. Place tog the two edges to be sewn.

2. Insert the tapestry needle, threaded with matching yarn, into the work, connecting the two pieces. Make certain to leave a tail to be weaved in so the sts do not unravel.

3. Draw the needle back around to the side into which the needle was first inserted and repeat Step 2.

4. Repeat Step 3 until entire edge is sewn.

5. Weave in yarn ends.

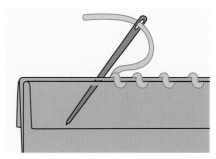

Fig. 47

Mattress Stitch (mattress st)

The mattress stitch is very easy to do and makes the seam between two pieces of stockinette fabrics nearly invisible.

1. Line up the two pieces to be sewn tog.

2. Using tapestry needle, pull the last st of the first row so that a horizontal bar appears.

3. Insert the tapestry needle underneath the horizontal bar, then under the parallel horizontal bar of the second piece (see Fig. 48).

4. Pull the yarn in the direction of the seam, not out. Make certain not to pull too tightly, as this may cause the fabrics to bunch tog.

5. Continue until entire seam is sewn.

Fig. 48

hats

Easy Beanie Hat

MATERIALS

- Needles, straight (size 8)
- Scissors
- Tapestry needle
- Yarn, worsted (120 yds)

GAUGE

5 sts = 1"

This hat is knit flat with a seam up the back. Much like the name implies, making this hat is so easy, you'll soon have one in every color. You will practice the stockinette stitch and learn to decrease by knitting two stitches together.

1. Co 84 sts. Refer to Casting On instructions on pages 17–18.

2. K for approximately 1". Refer to Garter (Knit) Stitch instructions on pages 19–20.

3. Switching to stockinette st, begin with a p row and work until piece measures 6". Refer to Purl Stitch instructions on page 21 and Stockinette Stitch instructions on page 22.

4. Beg dec as follows:

   Row 1: *K2tog, k5*. Repeat between *s 12 times through end of row, so 72 sts remain.

   Row 2: P one row.

   Row 3: *K2tog, k4*. Repeat between *s 12 times through end of row, so 60 sts remain.

   Row 4: P one row.

   Row 5: *K2tog, k3*. Repeat between *s 12 times through end of row, so 48 sts remain.

   Row 6: P one row.

   Row 7: *K2tog, k2*. Repeat between *s 12 times through end of row, so 36 sts remain.

   Row 8: P one row.

   Row 9: *K2tog, k1*. Repeat between *s 12 times through end of row, so 24 sts remain.

   Row 10: P one row.

   Row 11: *K2tog.* Repeat between *s 12 times through end of row, so 12 sts remain.

5. Cut yarn, leaving an 8" tail. Using tapestry needle, thread yarn through remaining 12 sts. Gather tightly and secure.

6. Continue, sewing back seam tog.

MATERIALS

- Needle, circular (size 15, 16" long)
- Needles, double-pointed (size 15)
- Scissors
- Stitch marker
- Tapestry needle
- Yarn, super bulky (approx. 55 yds)

GAUGE

2 sts = 1"

Rolled Brim Hat 1

In this project, you will be introduced to knitting in the round on both circular and double-pointed needles.

1. Co 42 sts on circular needle. Join in circle, being careful not to twist sts. Place marker at beg of rnd. Refer to Knitting in the Round on page 26.

2. K in the rnd for 6".

3. Beg dec as follows, switching to dp needle as necessary:

Rnd 1: K5, k2tog. Repeat around to marker.

Rnd 2: K4, k2tog. Repeat around to marker.

Rnd 3: K3, k2tog. Repeat around to marker.

Rnd 4: K2, k2tog. Repeat around to marker.

Rnd 5: K1, k2tog. Repeat around to marker.

Rnd 6: K2tog. Repeat around to marker so 6 sts remain on needle.

4. Cut yarn 3" long. Using tapestry needle thread yarn through remaining sts. Draw up tightly and secure.

Variation: For a flat brim, follow co instruction and work seed st or ribbing as shown in Seed Stitch Hat on page 52 for 3–4 rows, then k each rnd until piece measures 6". Continue with dec as above.

Rolled Brim Hat 2

MATERIALS

- Needle, circular (size 11, 16" long)
- Needles, double-pointed (size 11)
- Scissors
- Stitch marker
- Tapestry needle
- Yarn, bulky (approx. 80 yds)

GAUGE

2½–3 sts = 1"

Much like Rolled Brim Hat 1 on pages 36–37, this beanie incorporates the use of circular and double-pointed needles.

1. Co 64 sts on circular needle. Join in circle, being careful not to twist sts. Place marker at beg of rnd.

2. K in rnd 4".

3. Beg dec, changing to dp needles:

Rnd 1: K6, k2tog. Repeat around to marker.

Rnd 2: K5, k2tog. Repeat around to marker.

Rnd 3: K4, k2tog. Repeat around to marker.

Rnd 4: K3, k2tog. Repeat around to marker.

Rnd 5: K2, k2tog. Repeat around to marker.

Rnd 6: K1, k2tog. Repeat around to marker.

Rnd 7: K2tog. Repeat around to marker (6 sts on needles).

4. Cut yarn to 3" long. Using tapestry needle, thread yarn through remaining sts. Draw up tightly and secure.

Variation: For a flat brim, follow co instruction and work seed st or ribbing, as shown in Seed Stitch Hat on page 52, for 3–4 rows, then k each rnd until piece measures 6". Continue with dec as above.

Rolled Brim Hat 3

In this project, you will use smaller yarn in order to produce smaller stitches. This hat is the perfect topper for your little snow boy or girl.

1. Co 80 sts on circular needle. Join in circle, being careful not to twist sts. Place marker at beg of rnd.

2. K in rnd for 8" or desired length.

3. Beg dec, changing to dp needles:

Rnd 1: K6, k2tog. Repeat around to marker.

Rnd 2: K5, k2tog. Repeat around to marker.

Rnd 3: K4, k2tog. Repeat around to marker.

Rnd 4: K3, k2tog. Repeat around to marker.

Rnd 5: K2, k2tog. Repeat around to marker.

Rnd 6: K1, k2tog. Repeat around to marker.

Rnd 7: K2tog around remaining sts.

4. Cut yarn to 3" long. Using a tapestry needle, thread yarn through remaining sts. Draw up tightly and secure.

MATERIALS

- Needle, circular (size 11, 16" long)
- Needles, double-pointed (size 11)
- Scissors
- Stitch marker
- Tapestry needle
- Yarn, bulky (approx. 80 yds)

GAUGE

4 sts = 1"

For a different look, work a flat brim in k1 p1 ribbing for 1" and complete the pattern in garter stitch.

MATERIALS

- Needle, circular (size 7, 16" long)
- Needles, double-pointed (size 7)
- Scissors
- Stitch marker
- Tapestry needle
- Yarn, worsted (approx. 120 yds)

GAUGE

5 sts = 1"

Rolled Brim Hat 4

The smaller needle size used for this beanie will make your fingers far more nimble. The smaller yarn and smaller stitches will create a very fine stitch.

1. Co 96 sts on circular needle. Join in circle, being careful not to twist sts. Place marker at beg of rnd.

2. K in rnd for 6" or desired length.

3. Beg dec, changing to dp needles:

Rnd 1: K6, k2tog. Repeat around to marker.

Rnd 2: K5, k2tog. Repeat around to marker.

Rnd 3: K4, k2tog. Repeat around to marker.

Rnd 4: K3, k2tog. Repeat around to marker.

Rnd 5: K2, k2tog. Repeat around to marker.

Rnd 6: K1, k2tog. Repeat around to marker.

Rnd 7: K tog around so 12 sts remain.

4. Cut yarn to 3" long. Using tapestry needle, thread yarn through remaining sts. Draw up tightly and secure.

For a flat brim, follow co instructions and work ribbing or seed st, as shown in Seed Stitch Hat on page 52, for 3–4 rows, then k each rnd until piece measures 6". Continue with dec as directed above.

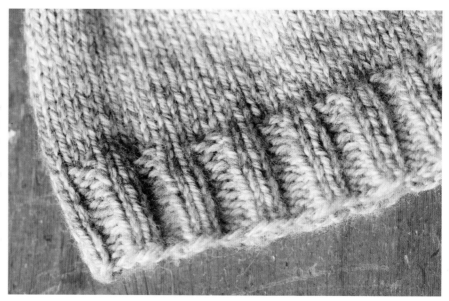

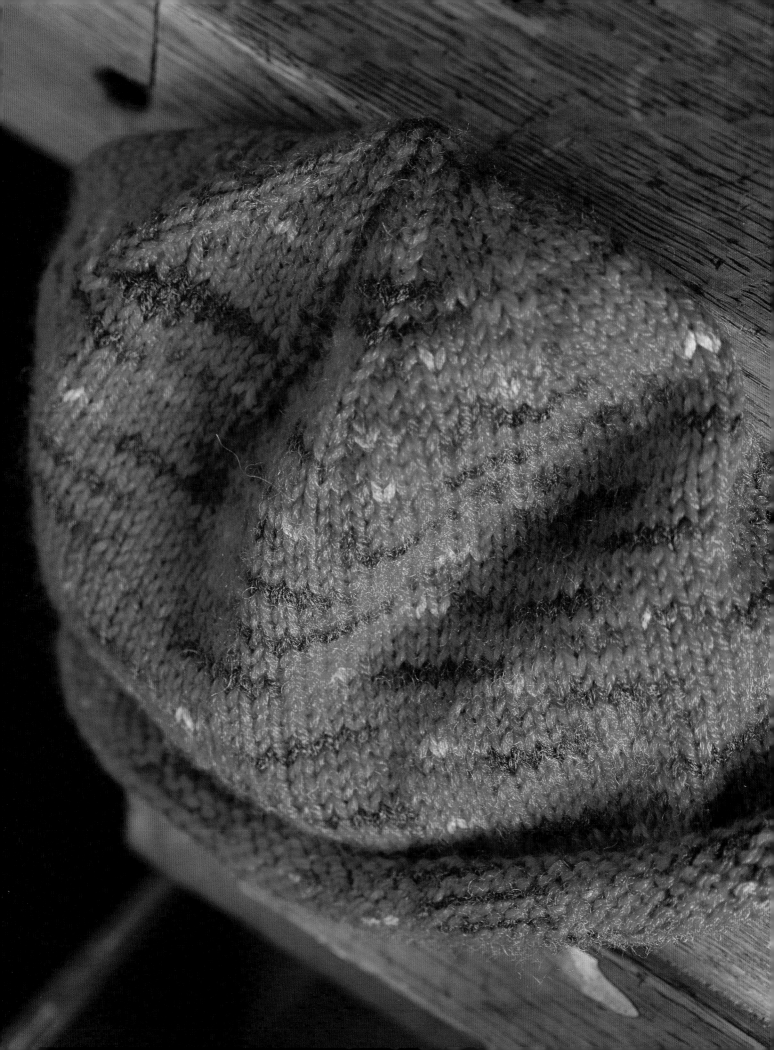

Alison's Two-stranded Hat

MATERIALS

- Needle, circular (size 9, 16" long)
- Needles, double-pointed (size 9)
- Scissors
- Stitch marker
- Tapestry needle
- Yarn, DK (200 yds each)

GAUGE

5 sts = 1"

The two-stranded hat is knit using two strands of yarn simultaneously. You can mix and match any variety of colors to create a fun, wild, or tame beanie that suits your personality alone.

1. With circular needle and two strands of yarn held tog, co 64 sts. Connect in the rnd, being careful not to twist sts, placing a marker to show beg of rnd.

2. K until hat measures 5½" from co edge.

3. Beg dec, changing to dp needles:

   Rnd 1: *K6, k2tog. Repeat from * all the way around.

   Rnd 2: K.

   Rnd 3: *K5, k2tog. Repeat from * all the way around.

   Rnd 4: K.

   Rnd 5: *K4, k2tog. Repeat from * all the way around.

   Rnd 6: K.

   Rnd 7: *K3, k2tog. Repeat from * all the way around.

   Rnd 8: K.

   Rnd 9: K2, k2tog. Repeat from * all the way around.

   Rnd 10: K.

   Rnd 11: K2 tog all the way around.

4. Cut tail. Using tapestry needle, thread yarn through remaining sts and secure on the inside of hat.

MATERIALS

- Crochet hook, large
- Needle, circular (size 6, 16" long)
- Scissors
- Stitch marker
- Yarn, cotton (110 yds)

GAUGE

5½ sts = 1"

Cotton Baby Beanie

This pattern offers versions for both boys and girls. The thin yarn and smaller needles might take a bit longer to knit the full hat; however, the recipient will look adorable.

BOY VERSION

1. Co 77 sts. Join in circle, being careful not to twist sts. Place marker at beg of rnd.

2. K until length measures 6½".

3. Beg dec:

Rnd 1: K1, k2tog. Repeat around.

Rnd 2: K2tog around.

4. Cut yarn to 18" long. Using crochet hook, thread yarn through all sts, and pull up tightly. Secure on inside of hat.

5. Weave in end of co yarn.

GIRL VERSION

1. Co 77 sts. Join in circle, being careful not to twist sts. Place marker at beg of rnd.

2. K 16 rnds (2").

3. Work six rnds in seed st.

4. K until length measures 6½".

5. Beg dec:

Rnd 1: K1, k2tog. Repeat around.

Rnd 2: K2tog around.

6. Cut yarn to 18" long. Using crochet hook, thread yarn through all sts, and pull up tightly. Secure on inside of hat.

7. Weave in end of co yarn.

MATERIALS

- Needle, circular (size 7, 16" long)
- Needles, double-pointed (size 7)
- Scissors
- Stitch marker
- Tapestry needle
- Yarn, worsted (approx. 120 yds) in 3 colors (1 main and 2 contrasts)

GAUGE

5 sts = 1"

Diamonds Hat

Creating patterns within a project may seem intimidating. Following this easy pattern will teach you to switch yarn colors mid-project, as well as alleviate any fears you may have about creating more complex projects.

1. Co 96 sts on circular needle. Join in circle, being careful not to twist sts. Place marker at beg of rnd.

2. K in ribbing of k1, p1 for 2".

3. Change to stockinette st for 2". Refer to Stockinette Stitch instructions on page 22.

4. Beg design:

    Rnd 1: K3 with main color, k1 with first contrast color.

    Rnd 2: K1 with main color, k3 with first contrast color.

    Rnd 3: K entire rnd with first contrast color.

    Rnd 4: K1 with main color, k3 with first contrast color.

    Rnd 5: K3 with main color, k1 with first contrast color.

    Rnd 6: K entire rnd with main color.

    Rnd 7: K3 with main color, k1 with second contrast color.

    Rnd 8: K1 with main color, k3 with second contrast color.

    Rnd 9: K entire rnd with second contrast color.

    Rnd 10: K1 with main color, k3 with second contrast color.

    Rnd 11: K3 with main color, k1 with second contrast color.

    Rnd 12: K entire rnd with main color.

    Rnd 13: K3 with main color, k1 with first contrast color.

    Rnd 14: K1 with main color, k3 with first contrast color.

    Rnd 15: K entire rnd with first contrast color.

    Rnd 16: K1 with main color, k3 with first contrast color.

    Rnd 17: K3 with main color, k1 with first contrast color.

5. Tie off contrasts and use only main color for dec.

6. Beg dec, changing to dp needles:

    Rnd 1: K6, k2tog. Repeat around to marker.

    Rnd 2: K5, k2tog. Repeat around to marker.

    Rnd 3: K4, k2tog. Repeat around to marker.

    Rnd 4: K3, k2tog. Repeat around to marker.

    Rnd 5: K2, k2tog. Repeat around to marker.

    Rnd 6: K1, k2tog. Repeat around to marker.

    Rnd 7: K2tog around so that 12 sts remain.

7. Cut yarn to 3" long. Using a tapestry needle, thread yarn through remaining sts. Draw up tightly and secure.

MATERIALS

- Needles, circular (size 2, 16" long)
- Needles, double-pointed (size 2)
- Scissors
- Stitch marker
- Yarn, "pattern making" sock yarn (110 yds)

GAUGE

7 sts = 1"

Action One-skein Hat

The sock yarn used in this project changes color often throughout the skein. The color repeat is very small, therefore it makes its own pattern.

1. Find a place where you have a long strand (about 1½ yds) of yarn in the same color to beg co. Co 140 sts on circular needle. Join in circle, making certain not to twist sts. Place marker at beg.

2. Beg ribbing by k2 p2, repeating all the way around to marker. Repeat this ribbing for 1½".

3. K until hat measures 5" or desired length.

4. Begin dec, changing to dp needles:

   Rnd 1: K8, k2tog. Repeat around to marker.

   Rnds 2–3: K.

   Rnd 4: K7, k2tog. Repeat around to marker.

   Rnds 5–6: K.

   Rnd 7: K6, k2tog. Repeat around to marker.

   Rnds 8–9: K.

   Rnd 10: K5, k2tog. Repeat around to marker.

   Rnds 11–12: K.

   Rnd 13: K4, k2tog. Repeat around to marker.

   Rnds 14–15: K.

   Rnd 16: K3, k2tog. Repeat around to marker.

   Rnds 17–18: K.

   Rnd 19: K2, k2tog. Repeat around to marker.

   Rnds 20–21: K.

   Rnd 22: K1, k2tog. Repeat around to marker.

   Rnd 23: K2tog. Repeat around to marker.

5. Cut yarn, leaving a long tail. Pull tail through all remaining sts. Pull tightly and weave in ends.

MATERIALS

- Needles, circular (size 7, 16" long)
- Scissors
- Yarn, worsted (200 yds per color) in 3 colors

GAUGE

5 sts = 1"

Seed Stitch Hat

This hat will help you practice the seed stitch as well as changing yarn colors mid-project. It is meant to match the Seed Stitch Scarf found on pages 62–63, so use any leftover yarn from this project for the scarf. *Note: When knitting in the round, start each new row making certain you are knitting the purl stitches and purling the knit stitches from the previous row.*

1. Co 96 sts with lightest color.

Rnd 1: K2, p2 and connect in the rnd.

Rnds 2–6: K2, p2 ribbing through end of sixth row.

Rnds 7–11: Switch to seed st and work to end of Row 11. Refer to Seed Stitch instructions on page 22.

Note: The remainder of the hat will be worked in seed st.

Rnds 12–13: Middle range color.

Rnds 14–15: Lightest color.

Rnds 16–17: Middle range color.

Rnds 18–19: Lightest color.

Rnds 20–27: Middle range color.

Rnds 28–29: Darkest color.

Rnds 30–31: Middle range color.

Rnds 32–33: Darkest color.

Rnds 34–35: Middle range color.

Rnds 36–45: Darkest color.

2. Beg dec:

Rnd 1: *Seed st 6 sts, K2tog*. Repeat around.

Rnd 2: Seed st. *Note: Sometimes 2 k or 2 p will show up due to the dec in the previous rnd. Although it will be difficult to make them look even, you can try.*

Rnd 3: Seed st 5 sts, k2tog. Repeat around so 70 sts remain.

Rnd 4: Seed st.

Rnd 5: Seed st 4 sts, k2tog. Repeat around so 48 sts remain.

Rnd 6: Seed st.

Rnd 7: Seed st 3 sts, k2tog. Repeat around so 30 sts remain.

3. Cut yarn and pull through remaining sts. Pull to inside of hat and secure.

scarves

MATERIALS

- Crochet hook
- Medium-weight cardboard, 9" × 3"–4" (2)
- Needles, straight (size 11)
- Plastic baggie
- Scissors
- Yarn, mohair blend (198 yds)

GAUGE

3½–4 sts = 1"

Easy Elegant Scarf

This project will teach you to create a simple fringe for embellishing scarves. Once you get the hang of it, this fringe technique can be applied to a variety of projects.

By creating the fringe first, the left-over yarn will be enough for a scarf width of 36 sts. However, if making the scarf before the fringe, make certain to set aside 36 yds of yarn to ensure enough remains.

1. Co 36 sts.
2. K all rows until desired length is reached.
3. Bo. Refer to Binding Off instructions on page 27.
4. Fold cardboard in half to measure 4½" × 3"–4" wide.
5. Wind yarn around 4½"-long side 72 times.
6. Slide one scissor blade into cardboard fold, cutting both cardboard and yarn. *Note: This will create 72 9" strands, or a four-strand 4½" fringe for each stitch along one end of the scarf.*
7. Place yarn strands into a plastic baggie.
8. Repeat Steps 4–7 for other end of scarf.
9. Fold two strands of fringe yarn in half, creating a lp. Using crochet hook, partially pull lp of fringe yarn through one original co st. Pull four strands of fringe through lp and pull tightly to create a knot.
10. Repeat across 35 remaining co sts.
11. Repeat across 36 sts at bo.

MATERIALS

- Crochet hook
- Needles, straight (size 35)
- Scissors
- Yarn, burly spun (132 yds)

GAUGE

2 sts = 1"

Wool Cabin Bulky Scarf

This basic scarf will teach you the slip stitch method for even edges. It is such a simple scarf, you will master it in no time.

1. Co 15 sts.

2. K desired number of rows, making certain to save enough yarn for a 15 st fringe width.

3. Sl the first st on every row. Refer to Slip Stitch instructions on page 22.

4. Bo.

5. Cut 30 9" strands of yarn for fringe.

6. Fold one strand of fringe yarn in half, creating a lp. Using crochet hook, partially pull lp of fringe yarn through one original co st. Pull the two strands of fringe through lp and pull tightly to create a knot.

7. Repeat across 14 remaining co sts.

8. Repeat across 15 sts at bo.

MATERIALS

- Needles, straight (size 15)
- Scissors
- Yarn, nylon ribbon (140 yds)
- Yarn, mohair (140 yds)

GAUGE

4 sts = 1"

Ribbon and Mohair Scarf

The combination of ribbon and mohair makes this scarf incredibly soft and silky. You will learn the yarn over method for creating small gaps or holes in order to produce a pattern.

1. Using both yarns tog, co 17 sts.

2. In seed st, k five rows.

Row 6: K1, yo. Refer to Yarn Over instructions on page 23. Repeat to end of row.

Row 7: K1, dropping the yo off needle. Repeat to end of row.

3. Repeat Step 2 until all yarn has been worked. *Note: Make certain to finish with five rows of seed st to ensure both ends of the scarf match.*

4. Bo.

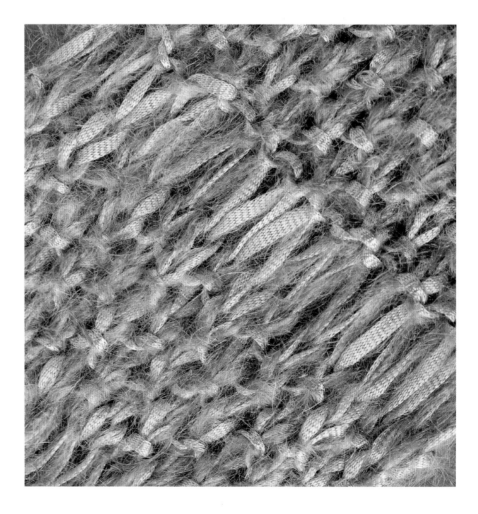

tip

Try hanging a safety pin or stitch marker on the side of the scarf on which the decrease, increase is knit. By doing so, the marker indicates which rows will decrease and increase. It's knitting without thinking!

Fun and Easy Bias Scarf

Visitors to the shop are always asking how I ever made this scarf. It is actually very easy and makes an interesting pattern.

1. Co 22 sts.

2. K one row.

3. K2tog, k19. Inc 1 st in last st, so there are 22 sts. Refer to Increasing instructions on page 23.

4. K one row.

5. Repeat Steps 3–4 until scarf is desired length.

6. Bo.

Let imagination be your guide when it comes to yarn for this project. A combination of novelty yarns in different colors and textures can create a different scarf every time.

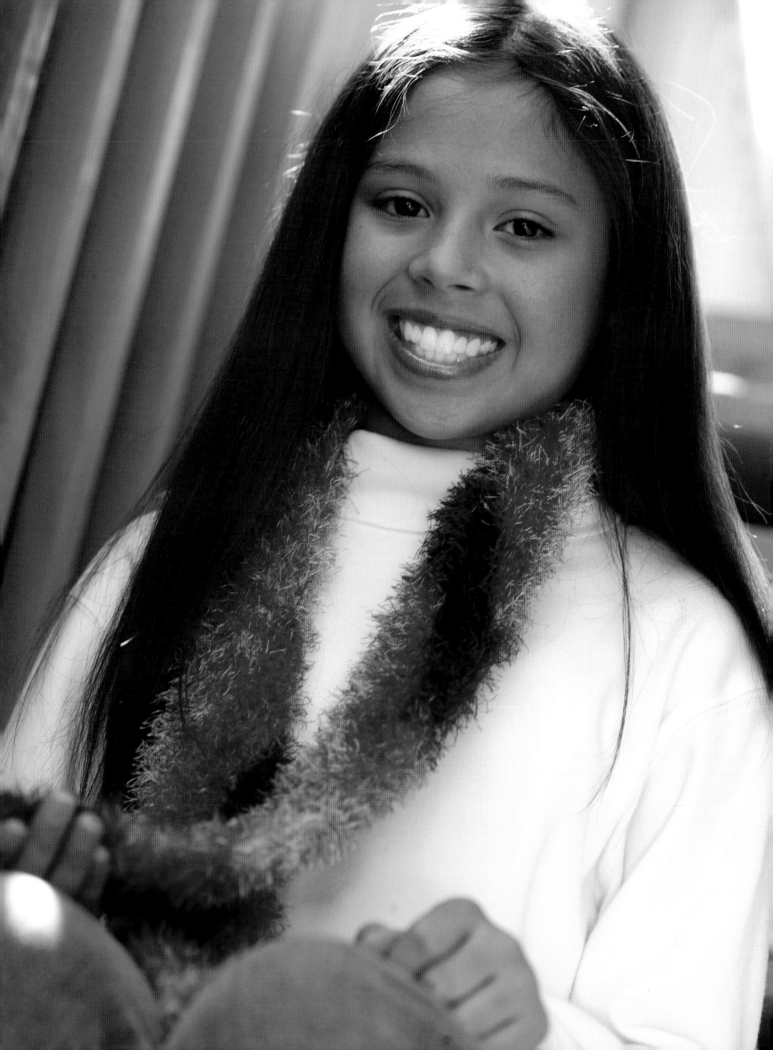

MATERIALS

- Needle, circular (size 7, 32" long)
- Scissors
- Yarn, worsted (200 yds per color) in 3 colors

GAUGE

5 sts = 1"

Seed Stitch Scarf

This striped scarf is knit lengthwise, teaching you to work with very long rows. To make the matching hat, refer to Seed Stitch Hat on page 52.

1. Co 300 sts, using darkest color.

2. Rnds 1–10: Seed st in darkest color.

3. K remainder of scarf in seed st, using the colors specified throughout instructions.

Rnds 11–12: Middle range color.

Rnds 13–14: Darkest color.

Rnds 15–16: Middle range color.

Rnds 17–18: Darkest color.

Rnds 19–26: Middle range color.

Rnds 27–28: Lightest color.

Rnds 29–30: Middle range color.

Rnds 31–32: Lightest color.

Rnds 33–34: Middle range color.

Rnds 35–36: Lightest color.

Rnds 37–38: Middle range color.

Rnds 39–48: Lightest color.

4. Bo.

MATERIALS

- Needles, straight (size 10½")*
- Scissors
- Yarns, novelty (approx. 150 yds per color/type) in 7 different colors and types

I recommend using a short, straight needle so you can see your work as you are knitting.

GAUGE

Depending on yarns used

Fabulous Novelty Scarf

This wonderful scarf can be made using novelty yarns that all have a "color theme" or you can use your "stash yarns." Creativity is the key—don't be afraid to try yarns that you wouldn't normally put together.

1. Line up yarns according to yardage. *Note: Knowing how much there is of each type of yarn will help you to determine which ones to use most often.*

2. Co 45 sts. Beg with a yarn that will make a good edge for a fringe. Make certain to save enough of this yarn for the other end. K 1½", or four rows.

3. Continue knitting scarf, switching yarns when desired. Make certain to k 1½", or four rows, with each yarn, tying in new yarns mid-row. *Note: Tying in yarns mid-row will create interesting knots in the work, as well as keep the edges even.*

4. Bo when scarf is 50" or desired length.

5. Cut 18" lengths of remaining yarn and tie tassels to scarf ends for fringe.

Feather and Fan Scarf

Knit by Lorrie Broman

This scarf will teach you to add a small border to this traditional pattern, achieving a graceful lacy fabric with a scalloped edge. There are two ways this project can be made: Option One is knit in two pieces, then joined at the center back of the neck, using the kitchener stitch; Option Two is knit all in one piece.

To make a narrower or wider scarf, cast on any multiple of 18, plus 6 stitches. Then follow the pattern instructions as usual.

Size: 8" × 56" (approx.)

MATERIALS

- Needles, straight (size 7)
- Scissors
- Stitch holder
- Yarn, 4-ply baby wool (540 yds)

GAUGE

7 sts = 1"

PATTERN
(used for both options)

1. Beg pattern:

   Row 1: K through end of row.

   Row 2: K3, p until 3 sts remain, k3.

   Row 3: K3, *k2tog three times, (yo, k1) six times, k2tog three times.* Repeat between *s, k3.

   Row 4: K through end of row.

OPTION ONE

1. Co 60 sts.

2. K two rows.

3. K Pattern instructions until piece measures 26" from co edge.

4. Place sts on holder, then cut yarn, leaving 30" for weaving seam. Set aside.

5. Repeat Steps 1–4 for second half of scarf.

6. Finish by seaming tog, using kitchener st. Refer to Kitchener Stitch instructions on page 23.

7. Weave in ends and block to shape.

OPTION TWO

1. Co 60 sts.

2. K two rows.

3. Repeat Pattern instructions until piece measures approximately 54" from co edge.

4. K two rows.

5. Bo loosely.

6. Weave in ends and block to shape.

bags

MATERIALS

- Decorative buttons
- Needle, circular (size 13, 24" long)
- Needles, double-pointed (size 10)
- Scissors
- Tapestry needle
- Yarns, wool that will felt, (450 yds) in main color, (150–200 yds) in contrast color depending on desired pocket size

GAUGE

5 sts = 1"

Felted Pocket Bag

This project teaches you to make pockets and will also teach you the I-cord method.

BAG

1. Co 100 sts of main color onto circular needle.

2. Join in the rnd, making certain not to twist sts. K in the rnd until piece measures 15" from co end.

3. Bo.

4. Fold bag flat and sew up co edge with tapestry needle.

POCKET

5. Co 40 sts of contrast color. *Note: Co more or fewer sts for a different size pocket.*

6. K all rows until pocket is 10" long.

7. Bo.

HANDLES

8. Co 5 sts of main color onto dp needles.

9. K handles in I-cord to desired length. Refer to I-cord instructions on page 33. *Note: Remember that felting usually shrinks the piece by at least one-third, so make certain to knit the handles long enough.*

10. Repeat Steps 8–9 to make second handle.

FINISHING

11. Felt all pieces. Refer to Felting instructions on page 32. Allow to dry.

12. Using tapestry needle and yarn, sew on pocket, handles, and decorative buttons.

My Knitting Bag

Now that you're a prolific knitter, you need a knitting bag to tote all those projects around with you. To avoid having the large knots on the outside of the felted bag, simply thread the handles backward so the knots end up on the inside.

MATERIALS

* Needle, circular (size 11, 32" long)
* Needles, double-pointed (size 10½)
* Scissors
* Stitch holder
* Stitch markers, 1 green and 3 red
* Yarns, 100% wool worsted weight, (700 yds) in main color, (150 yds) in contrast color

GAUGE

5 sts = 1"

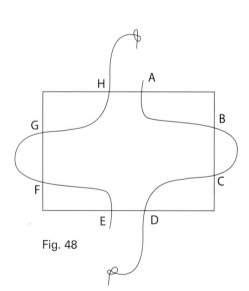

Fig. 48

BAG

1. Co 54 sts onto circular needle.

2. K 66 rows to make base. *Note: It is helpful to mark a self-adhesive note at the end of each row. It is much easier to count up slashes on the paper than to go back through the work to count rows.*

3. Place sts on holder.

4. Moving to one short side of the work, place the green marker on needle. Pick up and k32 sts along base piece, then place red marker.

5. Pick up and k54 sts along co edge, then place another red marker.

6. Pick up and k32 sts along second short side of the work, then place red marker.

7. K across 54 sts on holder.

8. K one rnd, sliding markers as necessary.

9. Repeat Step 8 until bag is 18" tall or desired height. *Note: As felting shrinks wool by about one-third, make certain knit piece is large enough.*

STRAP HOLES

10. Short side: K8, bo2, k12, bo2, k8.

11. Long side: K8, bo2, k34, bo2, k8.

12. Short side: Repeat Step 10.

13. Long side: Repeat Step 11.

14. On the next round, simply co 2 sts over the ones that were bo. *Note: This creates eight slots along the perimeter of the bag for the knit straps.*

15. P five rows to reinforce top edge of bag.

16. Bo.

STRAPS

17. Co 4 sts onto dp needle.

18. K in I-cord until tube is 60" long.

19. Repeat Steps 17–18 for second handle.

FINISHING

20. Felt all pieces.

21. Thread first handle into point A, out B, into C, and out D (see Fig. 48).

22. Thread second handle into point H, out G, into F, and out E.

23. Tie ends of handles together in square knots.

Alison's Fizzy Bag

This project will teach you to knit a flap for your bag without having to sew two separate pieces.

1. Co 26 sts, working two strands—one from each yarn—tog.

2. In seed st, k until piece measures 5". *Note: This will create the flap for the bag.*

3. Co an additional 50 sts at the end of last row. As there is no extra tail of yarn to co the extra sts, simply pull more yarn from the skein, creating a V to co more sts.

4. Join ends in the rnd; k all rows for 8".

5. Sew bottom tog using tapestry needle and yarn.

Color can define a mood or an attitude. When choosing a yarn color, think about the personality of the carrier of this bag and the occasions for which it will be used.

bags

MATERIALS

- Needle, circular (size 15, 24" long)
- Needles, double-pointed (size 11)
- Scissors
- Stitch markers, 1 green and 3 red
- Tapestry needle, large
- Yarn, novelty fringed (98 yds)
- Yarn, worsted (600 yds)

GAUGE

5 sts = 1"

Felted Fringe Bag

This bag was made with a special novelty fringe yarn. The yarn is all the same weight; however, there are a plethora of various colors, textures, and materials included in each skein. Because every skein is different, any project you choose to create will be completely unique and fun.

BAG

1. Beg bag at bottom, working two strands worsted yarn tog.

2. Co 30 sts onto circular needle.

3. Work 15 rows in stockinette st.

4. Co additional 60 sts and join in the rnd.

5. P one rnd.

6. P second rnd, adding red st markers at sts 30, 45, and 60. Add red marker after st 90. *Note: The green marker indicates the beginning of the round.*

7. Tie on novelty yarn and k all rnds until piece measures 12" from beg of novelty yarn or until it runs out.

8. P three rnds using worsted yarn.

9. Bo.

10. Using tapestry needle and yarn, whipstitch bottom to bag. Refer to Whipstitch instructions on page 33. Whipstitch bottom to sides and long edge of bag before felting.

HANDLES

11. With dp needles, co five sts with two strands of worsted yarn.

12. K in I-cord until piece measures 40".

13. Repeat Steps 11–12 for a second handle.

FINISHING

14. Felt all pieces.

15. Pinch sides of bag tog and insert handles into fold. Using tapestry needle and yarn, sew handles onto bag.

MATERIALS

- Button
- Needles, double-pointed (size 10½)
- Needles, straight (sizes 10½, 13)
- Scissors
- Tapestry needle
- Yarn, solid cotton/merino blend (382 yds)
- Yarn, tweed (191 yds)

GAUGE

5 sts = 1"

Garter Stitch Bag

This bag is knit flat, then sewn up the side seams for added stability. It will also give you more practice making the I-cord for a strap that is as long or short as you like.

BAG

1. Using two strands tweed and one strand solid yarn (three strands total), co 24 sts onto size 13 straight needle.

2. K all rows until tweed is used up, approximately 18", and tie off tweed.

3. Switch to size 10½ straight needles, and k four rows.

4. On next row, dec first and last sts; k all sts in between.

5. Repeat Step 4 until 2 sts remain.

6. Bo.

7. Using tapestry needle and yarn, sew up side seams.

HANDLE

8. Using one strand solid color, co 5 sts onto dp needle.

9. K in I-cord until 24" long, or to desired length.

10. Sew on handle and button.

A view of the inside of the Garter Stitch Bag reveals the consistency of the stitch.

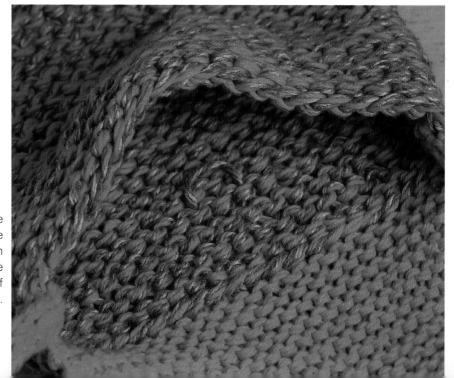

bags

MATERIALS

- Decorative buttons (4)
- Needle, circular (size 10½, 32" long)
- Needles, double-pointed (size 10½)
- Scissors
- Tapestry needle
- Yarn, worsted weight, (660 yds) in main color, (440 yds) in contrast color
- Yarn, multicolored rayon (408 yds)

GAUGE

5 sts = 1"

Alison's Felted Tote Bag

This project is fun and easy for beginning knitters. It will give you plenty of practice switching colors mid-project as well as with felting to the desired size.

Size before felting: 18" × 18"
Size after felting: 10½" × 15"

HANDLES

1. Using two strands of main color tog, co 2 sts onto dp needle.

Rnd 1: K.

Rnd 2: Inc both sts so there are 4 sts total.

Rnd 3: K.

Rnd 4: Inc first st, k to last st, inc in last st so there are 6 sts.

Rnds 5–9: K.

Rnd 10: K2tog, k2, k2tog.

2. Begin I-cord: Slide sts to the other end of the double points. Not turning needle, take yarn firmly across the back of the work and k4 sts. Repeat until strap is 35" long from co edge.

3. Inc first st, k2, inc last st so there are 6 sts.

4. K five rnds.

5. K2tog, k2, k2tog so there are 4 sts.

6. K2tog, k2tog.

7. K.

8. K last 2 sts tog.

9. Repeat Steps 1–8 for second handle.

Continued on page 81

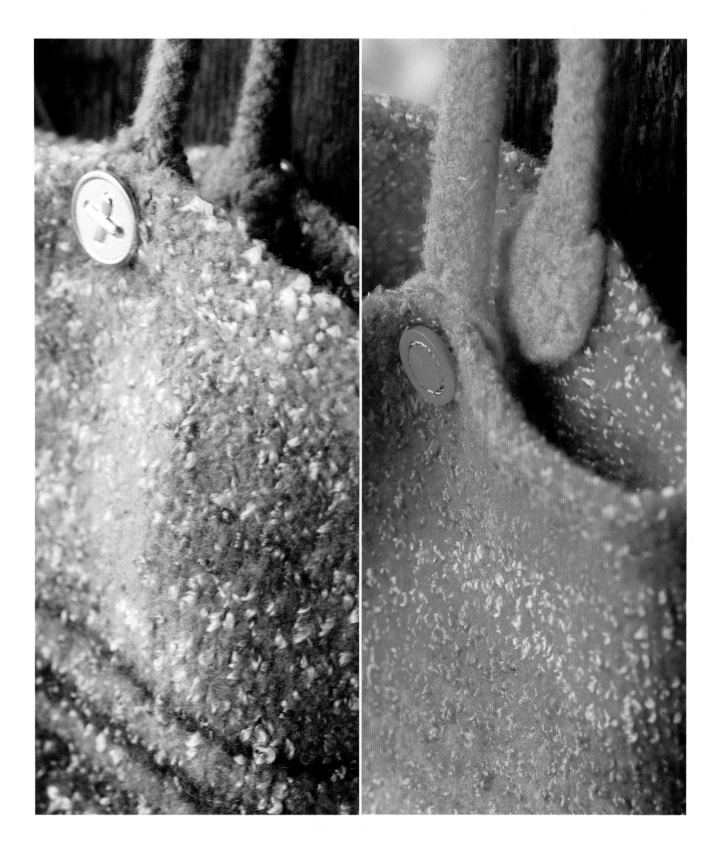

Continued from page 78

BAG

10. Using two strands of main color tog, co 48 sts onto circular needle.

11. Beg with side edge of work, pick up 24 sts. Turn and pick up 28 sts along next side, then 24 sts on last edge. Count the sts to make certain there are 144 sts on the needle.

12. Tie on multicolored yarn so that there are three strands being worked. *Note: Although initially this may seem intimidating, it is actually quite fun.*

13. Place marker before the first st. Connect work in the rnd and k all rnds until piece measures 9".

Rnd 1: K using contrast color and multicolored yarn.

Rnds 2–4: K using main color and multicolored yarn.

Rnds 5–6: K using contrast color and multicolored yarn.

Rnds 7–8: K using main color and multicolored yarn.

Rnds 9–11: K using contrast color and multicolored yarn.

Rnd 12: K using main color and multicolored yarn.

14. K several rnds using contrast color and multicolored yarn until piece measures 17".

15. P five rnds and bo.

FINISHING

16. Felt all three pieces. *Note: By first felting the knitted items, it will be easier to see the best area to place the handles.*

17. Using tapestry needle and yarn, sew handles to the inside of the bag. Sew buttons to the outside for decoration.

tip

Try cutting a piece of cardboard to fit the inside bottom of the tote, then sew it into place with the main color of yarn. This will give the bag a flat bottom.

blankets

MATERIALS
Option One
- Needle, circular (size 10, 29" long)
- Scissors
- Yarn, worsted (800 yds)

Option Two
- Needle, circular (size 7, 29" long)
- Scissors
- Yarn, DK weight (955 yds)

GAUGE
Option One
5 sts = 1"

Option Two
5½ sts = 1"

Wool Cabin Baby Blanket

This project will teach you to make a soft and snuggly baby blanket. There are two options available, so this pattern can result in different blankets for different babies. While the blankets are basically the same, the second variation will be more delicate, with smaller blocks.

PATTERN (used for both options)

1. Beg pattern:

Row 1: K all sts.

Row 2: K6, *p3, k1* until 9 sts remain. P3, k6.

Row 3: K all sts.

Row 4: K6, *p3, k1* until 9 sts remain. P3, k6.

Rows 5–6: K all sts.

OPTION ONE

1. Co 127 sts.

2. K 10 rows.

3. K Pattern instructions until 2" from final desired length.

4. K nine rows.

5. Bo.

OPTION TWO

1. Co 155 sts.

2. K 10 rows.

3. K Pattern instructions until 1½" from final desired length.

4. K nine rows.

5. Bo.

MATERIALS

- Needles, straight (size 10)
- Ribbon (optional)
- Scissors
- Yarn, plush (360 yds)

GAUGE

3 sts = 1"

Plush Baby Blanket

This blanket is knit from corner to corner instead of in a regular square. It will offer plenty of practice increasing through the yarn-over method, and decreasing by knitting two stitches together.

1. Co 5 sts.

2. K2, yo, k remainder of row.

3. Repeat Step 2 until two skeins of yarn have been used, or blanket is half the desired size.

4. Beg dec as follows:

K1, k2tog, yo, k2tog, k remainder of row.

5. Repeat Step 4 until 5 sts remain on needle.

6. Bo.

7. Optional: Weave ribbon through holes on border.

A blue striped ribbon woven around the edge adds a colorful detail to this creamy white blanket.

MATERIALS

- Needles, straight (size 8)
- Scissors
- Yarn, worsted weight
  (2 skeins each) in 5 colors

GAUGE

5 sts = 1"

tip

Be creative in assembling your squares. They need not be in any particular order. Even our stitches ran both vertically and horizontally.

Knit Together Afghan

Assembly and Crochet Edging by Deb Rigby

It can be great fun to work on a "community" knitting project. Each person works on a portion of the piece, then the sections are sewn or knit together to create one large item.

This afghan was created by a group of women who go on a knitter's retreat each year. Everyone takes a few minutes to knit a few squares before assembling the blanket, which is then donated to a charitable organization.

There are a few different ways that you can undertake this type of project. A great way to use up stash yarn or leftovers, of which there is too much to throw out but not enough for a whole project, is to have each person in the group knit a few random squares. Using stash yarn, however, can make it difficult to achieve squares of uniform size, which then causes trouble when it is time to knit them together. Another way to accomplish a Knit Together Afghan is to decide on a theme, and use the same yarn. Pastels, bright colors, or a rainbow can all produce beautiful results.

This blanket was the last piece my mother worked on, so I cherish it each time I wrap myself in it.

1. Co 30 sts and k 30 rows.

2. Repeat Step 1 until all yarn has been used. *Note: Our afghan resulted in 11 yellow, 11 purple, 11 green, 14 blue, and 9 pink squares.*

MATERIALS

- Cable needle
- Needle, circular (size 8, 29" long)
- Safety pin
- Scissors
- Stitch markers
- Tapestry needle
- Yarn, DK weight (1,030 yds)

GAUGE

5½ sts = 1"

Cables and Lace Baby Afghan

Designed by Monica Karlson Atkin

This blanket introduces you to cabling. Although it may seem intimidating at first, cabling is quite easy once you get the hang of it. There are several variations, so each time you choose to make this project, it can turn out a little bit differently.

Size: approx. 37" x 41" after blocking

1. Co 163 sts.

Rows 1–9: K.

Row 10: Place a safety pin along this edge to indicate RS. K6, place marker, p1, *k6, yo, ssk, k, k2tog, yo. Refer to Slip, Slip, Knit instructions on page 24. Repeat from * until 13 sts remain. K6, p1, place marker, k6.

Row 11: K7, p to last 7 sts, k7.

Row 12: K6, place marker, p1, *k6, k1, yo, sl1, k2tog, yo. Repeat from * until 13 sts remain. K6, p1, place marker, k6.

Row 13: Repeat Row 11.

Row 14: K6, place marker, p1, *k6, yo, ssk, k1, k2tog, yo. Repeat from * until 13 sts remain. K6, p1, place marker, k6.

Row 15: Repeat Row 11.

Row 16: K6, place marker, p1, *fc3, k1, yo, sl1, k2tog, psso, yo, k1. Refer to Cable instructions and Pass Slip Stitch Over instructions on page 24. Repeat from * until 13 sts. remain. Fc3, p1, k6.

Row 17: Repeat Row 11.

Rows 18–25: Repeat Rows 10–17 until afghan measures approximately 38".

Rows 26–33: K.

2. Bo loosely.

Variation One: Work Rows 1–9 and Rows 26–33 as well as the first and last 6 sts of each row in seed st for an alternate border.

Variation Two: Substitute bc for fc to change the direction of the cables, or alternate between fc and bc each time Row 16 is repeated.

Variation Three: For a full-size afghan, co 195 sts, work the pattern for 57", k eight rows, then bo.

ponchos and shawls

MATERIALS

- Needles, straight (size 7)
- Scissors
- Tapestry needle
- Yarn, cotton (648 yds)

GAUGE

4 sts = 1"

Cotton Poncho

This poncho is very easy to make, as it is knit completely flat. It is then sewn up one side, leaving an opening for your head. Easy and chic, it doesn't get any better than this!

1. Co 109 sts.
   Row 1: *K1, yo, k2tog, p1.* Repeat to end of row.
   Row 2: *P1, yo, p2tog, k1.* Repeat to end of row.

2. Repeat Rows 1–2 until piece measures 50".

3. Bo.

4. Lay in a horseshoe shape. Using tapestry needle and yarn, sew up one side, leaving opening for head.

5. Optional: Add fringe if desired.

MATERIALS

- Needles, straight (size 17 or 11)
- Yarn, cotton/nylon ribbon (300 yds) or bulky rayon (274 yds), plus 75 yds for fringe (optional)

GAUGE

Depending on yarn and needle used

Narrow Shawl

This pattern makes an elegant shawl that looks great draped over a summer dress. It simply requires knitting and increasing, so it can be made quickly.

1. Co 45 sts.

2. Inc first st, k through row, inc last st.

3. Repeat Step 2 until project is desired width.

4. Bo.

5. Optional: Add fringe if desired.

Long-eyelash cotton/nylon ribbon yarn gives a fringed look to this variation of the Narrow Shawl.

Rectangles Poncho

The basic rectangles are simple to shape; however, the method for connecting the two pieces creates an intriguing piece that can be worn with the triangle to the front, or off to the side for a squared-off front. It will also teach you to sew two pieces together using the mattress stitch, which will make a nearly invisible seam.

MATERIALS

- Needle, straight (size 11)
- Scissors
- Sewing needle
- Straight pins
- Tapestry needle
- Yarn, any that will give you 4 sts per inch

GAUGE

4 sts = 1"

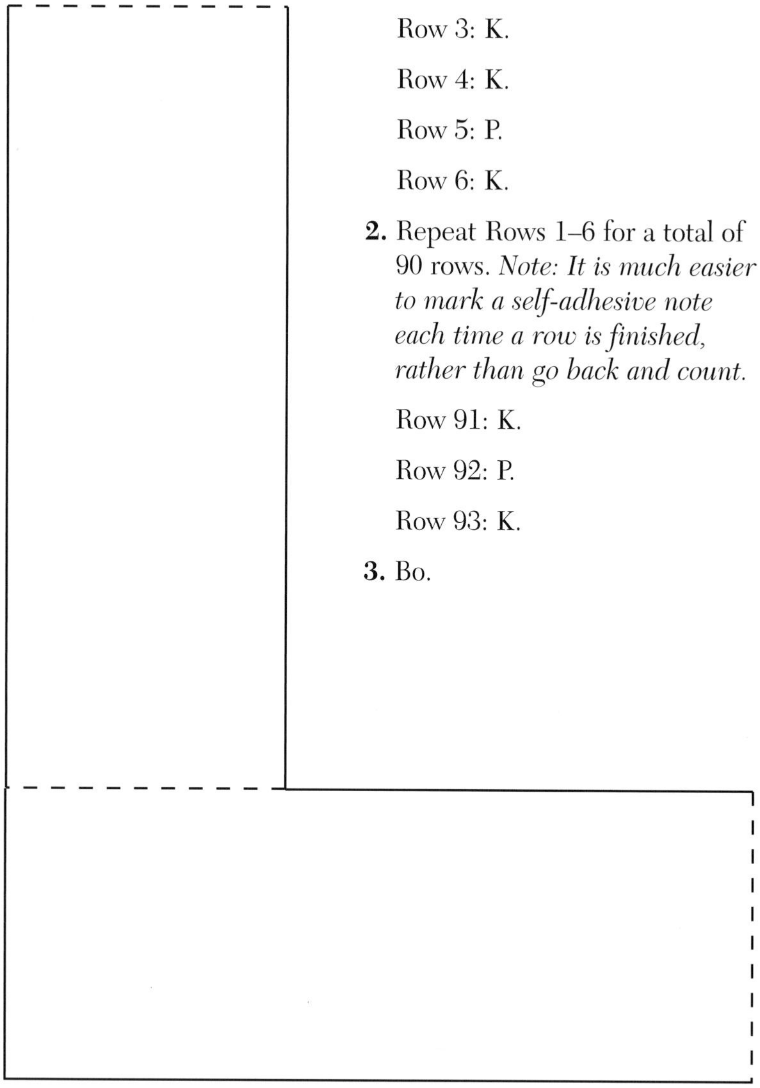

Fig. 49

1. Make two rectangles as follows: Co 88 sts.

Row 1: K.

Row 2: P.

Row 3: K.

Row 4: K.

Row 5: P.

Row 6: K.

2. Repeat Rows 1–6 for a total of 90 rows. *Note: It is much easier to mark a self-adhesive note each time a row is finished, rather than go back and count.*

Row 91: K.

Row 92: P.

Row 93: K.

3. Bo.

ASSEMBLY

4. Lay rectangles out flat with one short edge lined up against one long edge (see Fig. 49, central dotted line). Insert pins 12" in from edge to hold the two pieces tog.

5. Using tapestry needle and yarn, sew the two pieces tog with mattress st. Refer to Mattress Stitch instructions on page 33.

6. Pin the remaining edges (remaining dotted lines) of the rectangle tog. Sew the pieces tog.

MATERIALS

- Buttons (4 [5, 6])
- Needle, circular (size 7)
- Needles, double-pointed (size 7 or size to get gauge)
- Ring markers (6)
- Tapestry needle
- Yarn, worsted weight (300 [500, 700] yds)

GAUGE

5 sts = 1"

Monica's Easy Baby Sweater

Designed by Monica Scazzare

This is an easy sweater that requires almost no finishing. There are two variations for the collar—a fancy collar or a simple garter stitch, and two options for increases—decorative eyelets or simple and sleek. You can mix and match details to create a sweater as unique as the baby it's knit for.

Sizes: 6–12 months (1–2 years, 3–4 years)

SIMPLE COLLAR VARIATION

1. Co 62 (70, 78) sts.

2. K four (six, eight) rows.

3. Next row: Make buttonhole and set raglan shaping.

For boys (RS): K1, k2tog, yo, k2, place marker, k8 (10, 11), inc in next st, place marker, inc in next st, k6 (7, 8), inc in next st, place marker, inc in next st, k16 (18, 22), inc in next st, place marker, inc in next st, k6 (7, 8), inc in next st, place marker, inc in next st, k8 (10, 11), place marker, k5.

For girls (RS): K5, place marker, k8 (10, 11), inc in next st, place marker, inc in next st, k6 (7, 8), inc in next st, place marker, inc in next st, k16 (18, 22), inc in next st, place marker, inc in next st, k6 (7, 8), inc in next st, place marker, inc in next st, k8 (10, 11), place marker, k2, yo, k2tog, k1.

4. Next row: K5, p to last marker, k5.

5. Next row: K5, sl marker, *k to first st before next marker, inc in next st, sl marker, inc in next st. Repeat from * three times. K through end of row. *Note: Make certain piece has inc by 8 sts 78 (86, 94).*

6. Next row: K5, p to last marker, k5.

7. Repeat Steps 4–6, inc as set and working a buttonhole.

For boys: K1, k2tog, yo, k2 on the right side of the button band every 10 garter-st ridges until there are 190 (214, 254) sts total.

For girls: K2, yo, k2tog, k1 on the left side of the button band every 10 garter-st ridges until there are 190 (214, 254) sts total.

8. Work two rows even.

Continued on page 98

DIVIDE FOR FIRST SLEEVE

9. K across first 30 (34, 39) sts and leave on circular needles.

10. Using dp needles, k across next 40 (45, 54) sts. Evenly divide onto dp needles.

11. Place marker and join in the rnd.

Rnds 1–5: K.

Rnd 6: K1, k2tog, k to 3 sts before marker, ssk, k1.

Repeat Rnds 1–6 until piece measures 5½" (6½", 7½") from the dividing row.

Next rnd: P entire round, dec to 30 (33, 36) sts if necessary.

Next rnd: K entire round.

Repeat last two rnds until there are three garter-st ridges, making certain to end on a k row.

12. P to bo.

DIVIDE FOR SECOND SLEEVE

13. Rejoin yarn and work across next 50 (56, 58) sts. Leave sts on needle.

14. Using dp needles, k across next 40 (45, 54) sts. Evenly divide onto dp needles.

15. Place marker and join in the rnd.

Rnds 1–5: K.

Rnd 6: K1, k2tog, k to 3 sts before marker, ssk, k1.

Repeat Rnds 1–6 until piece measures 5½" (6½", 7½") from the dividing row.

Next rnd: P entire round, dec to 30 (33, 36) sts if necessary.

Next rnd: K entire round.

Repeat last two rnds until there are three garter-st ridges, making certain to end on a k row.

16. P to bo.

17. Rejoin yarn and k remaining sts on dividing row. *Note: Do not forget to make the buttonholes on the appropriate side after every 10 garter-st ridges.*

18. Next row: K5, p until 5 sts remain, k5.

BODY

19. K across row.

20. K5, p until 5 sts remain, k5.

21. Repeat Steps 19–20 until 4 (5, 6) buttonholes have been worked or garment is desired length.

22. K seven rows in garter st, ending on a RS row.

23. Co knitwise.

24. Using tapestry needle and yarn, weave in all ends, secure gap at underarm, if needed. Sew on buttons and block, if needed.

FANCY INCREASE VARIATION

To create a fancier sweater, substitute k1, yo for inc in st following the markers throughout pattern.

Continued on page 100

The Fancy Increase Variation on this baby sweater creates charming eyelets that line the raglan sleeves.

FANCY COLLAR VARIATION

1. Co 52 (60, 68) sts and work in garter st for 2½", (2½", 3"), ending after a RS row.

Row 1 (WS): K4, k2tog until 4 sts remain, k4. *Note: This should leave 30 (34, 38) sts remaining.*

Row 2 (RS): K4, p to last 4, k4.

Row 3: K.

Row 4: K4, p to last 4, k4.

Row 5: K4, k into the front and back of the next 22 (26, 30) sts, k4 (52, 60, 68 sts).

Row 6: K4, p to last 4, k4.

2. Make buttonhole and set raglan shaping.

Row 1: Co 5 additional sts at the beg of the row for the left button band, place marker, k8 (10, 11) inc in next st, place marker, inc in next st, k6 (7, 8) inc in next st, place marker, inc in next st, k16 (18, 22) inc in next st, place marker, inc in next st, k6 (7, 8) inc in next st, place marker, inc in next st k8 (10, 11) place marker, k5.

Row 2: Co 5 additional sts at the beg of the row for the right button band, place marker, p to last marker, k5.

For boys (RS): The buttonhole is on the left band. K1, k2tog, yo, k2, sl marker, *k to 1 st before next marker, inc in the next st, sl marker, inc in the next st. Repeat from * three times. K to end of row. (78 [86, 94] sts on needles)

For girls (RS): The buttonhole is on the right band. K5, sl marker, *k to 1 st before next marker, inc in the next st, sl marker, inc in the next st. Repeat from * three times. K to end of row. (78 [86, 94] sts on needles) *Note: You have inc eight sts.*

Next row: K5, p to last marker, k5.

3. Complete sweater following Steps 8–24 for Simple Collar Variation on pages 96–99.

MATERIALS

- 14" pillow form
- Buttons
- Needles, straight (size 8)
- Scissors
- Tapestry needle
- Yarn, worsted weight, contrast color (200 yds)
- Yarn, worsted weight, main color (200 yds)

GAUGE

5 sts = 1"

Wool Cabin Pillow

This pillow cover incorporates both seed stitch and stockinette stitch to create a varied look. It requires no finishing because it is sewn in one piece and folded in half, then the flap is folded over the front.

1. Co 60 sts main color.

2. Work in stockinette st for 7".

3. Switching to contrast color, work five rows in seed st.

4. Switching to main color, work four rows in stockinette st.

5. Repeat Steps 3–4 four times, ending with seed st.

6. Switching to main color, work in stockinette st for 14".

7. Cut main color, join contrast color and work k2, p2 ribbing for 7".

8. Bo in k2, p2 ribbing.

9. Weave in ends. Fold pieces after last seed-st pattern at the bottom and sew front and back tog.

10. Insert pillow form, fold ribbed flap down, sew seams with flap over, and sew on buttons.

Sunflower buttons add a cheerful touch to this green and yellow version of the Wool Cabin Pillow.

MATERIALS

- Needles, straight (size 8)
- Scissors
- Tapestry needle
- Yarn, cotton (80 yds)

GAUGE

5 sts = 1"

Knitted Round Dishcloth

This project will teach you to make a scalloped edge along the perimeter of a round project. Although it is a dishcloth, it might just be too pretty to use in the kitchen.

1. Co 15 sts.

Row 1: K.

Row 2: K3, yo, k11 so 1 st remains.

Row 3: K.

Row 4: K3, yo, k11 so 2 sts remain.

Row 5: K.

Row 6: K3, yo, k11 so 3 sts remain.

Row 7: K.

Row 8: Bo 3 sts to create the first scallop, k2, yo, k8 so 4 sts remain.

Row 9: K.

Row 10: K3, yo, k8 so 5 sts remain.

Row 11: K.

Row 12: K3, yo, k8 so 6 sts remain.

Row 13: K.

Row 14: Bo 3 sts, k2, yo, k5 so 7 sts remain.

Row 15: K.

Row 16: K3, yo, k5 so 8 sts remain.

Row 17: K.

Row 18: K3, yo, k5 so 9 sts remain.

Row 19: K.

Row 20: Bo 3 sts, k to end of row.

2. Repeat Rows 1–20 until there are seven patterns.

3. Bo. Using tapestry needle, draw up to center and sew.

MATERIALS

- Needle, circular (size 13, 32" long)
- Scissors
- Tapestry needle
- Yarn, 100% wool (approx. 3,600 yds) in various colors

GAUGE

5 sts = 1"

Circular Rug

This project will teach you to make a felted rug. It is composed of 18 sections, which can be any colors you like. Each wedge requires 200 yds of yarn, which is generally about one skein. The rug is knit in one large piece, using short rows. It is worked from the center out, joining with one seam to finish.

I used two skeins each of eight solid colors, one skein of the ninth solid color, two skeins each of eight tweed colors, and one skein of the ninth tweed color to make my rug. I wound the two skeins of like colors together and halved the single skeins before rewinding into a single ball for added thickness. By following the pattern, you will know exactly when to quit so that you have enough yarn for the other wedge of that color.

1. Panel pattern: Co 80 sts.

Row 1 and all odd rows: K.

Row 2: K10, yo, k67, turn so 3 sts remain.

Row 4: K10, yo, k65, turn so 6 sts remain.

Row 6: K10, yo, k63, turn so 9 sts remain. *Note: Each time the work is turned, there will be 3 more sts on the needle than the previous row.*

Row 8: K10, yo, k61, turn.

Row 10: K10, yo, k59, turn.

Row 12: K10, yo, k57, turn.

Row 14: K10, yo, k55, turn.

Row 16: K10, yo, k53, turn.

Row 18: K10, yo, k51, turn.

Row 20: K10, yo, k49, turn.

Row 22: Bo 10 sts, k9, yo, k37, turn.

Row 24: K10, yo, k35, turn.

Row 26: K10, yo, k33, turn.

Row 28: K10, yo, k31, turn.

Row 30: K10, yo, k29, turn.

Row 32: K10, yo, k27, turn.

Row 34: K10, yo, k25, turn.

Row 36: K10, yo, k23, turn.

Row 38: K10, yo, k21, turn.

Row 40: K10, yo, k19, turn.

Row 41: Bo 10 sts, k through end of row. Make certain there are once again 80 sts on the needle.

2. Repeat Rows 1–41 until 18 panels have been completed.

3. Using tapestry needle and yarn, sew seam to close circle and tie center circle closed.

4. Weave in all ends.

5. Wash 2–3 times to felt, checking often.

6. Stretch out on floor, stretching as necessary to shape. Allow to air dry.

The author (seated) with her husband, six children, and son-in-law on the day of her daughter's wedding.

The author's mother, Renee Edwards Groves.

AFTERWORD

Since I became a knitter, I have found that knitting has been a constant source of strength and joy throughout all the difficult times in my life. Knitting became my solace in the summer of 1997, when my sister Aimee took her own life in a beautiful Utah canyon. The aftermath of her death created one of the most trying periods in my life. I cannot imagine living through it without the calming rhythm of my needles.

Today, as one of the owners of the Wool Cabin, I realize how great an experience it was working with my mom at the shop. A few years after her passing, I find it hard to believe our little shop has come so far. I never could have made it without the support and encouragement of my husband Al. We have six wonderful children; the three youngest, Sarah, Joe, and Sam, are at home. My three oldest children, Zack, Rachel, and Garrett, are now on their own. Rachel is married to a wonderful man named Dan, and perhaps they will soon give me a grandchild to knit for.

Knitting is such a precious gift that the women in my family have given me, and one that I hope to give my daughters. I hope that you have found something in this book to inspire you, help you relax, and bond you to the many wonderful knitters such as those I get to meet every day.

DEDICATION

This book is dedicated to my mom, Renee Edwards Groves, who taught me to be strong in the face of adversity, that I can accomplish anything, and that knitting can soothe my troubled heart. I'll see you in heaven. Love, Ally

ACKNOWLEDGMENTS

As I reflect back on the wonderful process of creating this book, I must thank my sister Suzette Cannon and my brother Alex Groves. They have been so supportive and patient as we have faced incredible obstacles together. Thank you for keeping the Wool Cabin and your crazy sister on the right track! I love you both!

Metric Equivalency Chart

mm-millimeters   cm-centimeters
inches to millimeters and centimeters

inches	mm	cm	inches	cm	inches	cm
⅛	3	0.3	9	22.9	30	76.2
¼	6	0.6	10	25.4	31	78.7
½	13	1.3	12	30.5	33	83.8
⅝	16	1.6	13	33.0	34	86.4
¾	19	1.9	14	35.6	35	88.9
⅞	22	2.2	15	38.1	36	91.4
1	25	2.5	16	40.6	37	94.0
1¼	32	3.2	17	43.2	38	96.5
1½	38	3.8	18	45.7	39	99.1
1¾	44	4.4	19	48.3	40	101.6
2	51	5.1	20	50.8	41	104.1
2½	64	6.4	21	53.3	42	106.7
3	76	7.6	22	55.9	43	109.2
3½	89	8.9	23	58.4	44	111.8
4	102	10.2	24	61.0	45	114.3
4½	114	11.4	25	63.5	46	116.8
5	127	12.7	26	66.0	47	119.4
6	152	15.2	27	68.6	48	121.9
7	178	17.8	28	71.1	49	124.5
8	203	20.3	29	73.7	50	127.0

yards to meters

yards	meters	yards	meters	yards	meters	yards	meters	yards	meters
⅛	0.11	2⅛	1.94	4⅛	3.77	6⅛	5.60	8⅛	7.43
¼	0.23	2¼	2.06	4¼	3.89	6¼	5.72	8¼	7.54
⅜	0.34	2⅜	2.17	4⅜	4.00	6⅜	5.83	8⅜	7.66
½	0.46	2½	2.29	4½	4.11	6½	5.94	8½	7.77
⅝	0.57	2⅝	2.40	4⅝	4.23	6⅝	6.06	8⅝	7.89
¾	0.69	2¾	2.51	4¾	4.34	6¾	6.17	8¾	8.00
⅞	0.80	2⅞	2.63	4⅞	4.46	6⅞	6.29	8⅞	8.12
1	0.91	3	2.74	5	4.57	7	6.40	9	8.23
1⅛	1.03	3⅛	2.86	5⅛	4.69	7⅛	6.52	9⅛	8.34
1¼	1.14	3¼	2.97	5¼	4.80	7¼	6.63	9¼	8.46
1⅜	1.26	3⅜	3.09	5⅜	4.91	7⅜	6.74	9⅜	8.57
1½	1.37	3½	3.20	5½	5.03	7½	6.86	9½	8.69
1⅝	1.49	3⅝	3.31	5⅝	5.14	7⅝	6.97	9⅝	8.80
1¾	1.60	3¾	3.43	5¾	5.26	7¾	7.09	9¾	8.92
1⅞	1.71	3⅞	3.54	5⅞	5.37	7⅞	7.20	9⅞	9.03
2	1.83	4	3.66	6	5.49	8	7.32	10	9.14

Index